Guiding Adolescent Readers to Success

Authors

Mark Donnelly and Julie Donnelly

Foreword

Catherine Reischl, Ph.D.

SHELL EDUCATION

Publishing Credits

Dona Herweck Rice, *Editor-in-Chief*; Lee Aucoin, *Creative Director*;
Don Tran, *Print Production Manager*; Timothy J. Bradley, *Illustration Manager*;
Sara Johnson, M.S.Ed., *Senior Editor*; Hillary Wolfe, *Editor*;
Juan Chavolla, *Interior Layout Designer*; Corinne Burton, M.A.Ed., *Publisher*

Shell Education

5301 Oceanus Drive
Huntington Beach, CA 92649-1030
http://www.shelleducation.com

ISBN 978-1-4258-0828-0

©2012 Shell Educational Publishing, Inc.
Reprinted 2013

Table of Contents

Foreword

Let me introduce you to two people you'd love to have teaching across the hall from you. Julie and Mark Donnelly, authors of *Guiding Adolescent Readers to Success,* are down-to-earth, funny, and high-energy people. As a teaching couple who made the transition from the world of business into education almost 10 years ago, the Donnellys are enveloped in their work. They laugh about sharing questioning strategies with each other as they clean up the nightly dinner dishes or talk through ideas for addressing key themes in *The Watsons Go To Birmingham—1963* as they drive their own kids to school. They serve on district Language Arts committees, collaborate with colleagues to overhaul the middle school curriculum, and regularly work with beginning teachers and university teacher educators, such as myself, to question and hone their own teaching practices. They celebrate when summer vacation arrives and then work their way through a stack of young adult novels as the weeks slip by. In short, Julie and Mark are the kind of committed teaching professionals who truly work to make a difference in the lives of kids.

In this book, the Donnellys have pooled their experiences and professional knowledge and generously offer their teaching colleagues a practical guide to engaging middle school kids in meaningful reading instruction. Julie and Mark are teachers who "get it," who live within the limits of teaching 100–150 adolescents a day, yet have designed literacy instruction that is both doable and that leads to measureable success for the full range of 6th through 8th graders that walk through the classroom door.

Read this book to learn how to plan for and manage class periods where kids lose themselves in novels and are startled when the bell rings. Read this book to learn how to create a classroom culture that communicates such high expectations of 7th graders that they readily read one book at school while simultaneously working through another at home and can argue with a friend about common themes across the texts. Read this book to learn how to flexibly adjust your own questioning strategies to include English language learners and students with special needs in thoughtful conversations about text that move beyond the literal. And, read this book to remind yourself that adolescents are inherently interesting people for whom reading can be a huge resource as they explore their beliefs, ideas, and relationships.

Finally, read and enjoy this book, and consider what features of your own literacy teaching you might share with colleagues—whether in short bursts of conversation with a friend at the copy machine, in sharing a unit of lesson plans with your grade level group, or in composing a careful description of a particular set of teaching practices and grounding this work in research, such as Julie and Mark Donnelly have done here. These are the moves that build our profession and assist us to teach a broad range of children to use language and literacy in meaningful ways.

Catherine H. Reischl, Ph.D.
Clinical Associate Professor of Education
University of Michigan-Ann Arbor

Acknowledgements

This adolescent guided reading program is a success because of the incredibly intellectual and giving educators with whom we have been fortunate to work. Our initial inspiration to teach literacy stemmed from classes we took from Dr. Catherine Reischl, an amazing teacher who continually reminded us of the need to reach every student. When we began to build our genre carts (book collections), Michelle Rodriguez, our media specialist, always handed us the perfect book for our lessons. Chuck Hatt, our district's curriculum leader, championed the implementation of our adolescent guided reading program throughout the entire district. He enthusiastically trained teachers and supported us with endless encouragement. Linda Prieskorn, our good friend and master teacher, critiqued our earliest versions of this book and motivated us to expand our ideas beyond our own classrooms. Finally, thank you to all the extraordinary language arts teachers who incorporated this guided reading program into their classrooms.

We are also extremely grateful for the efforts of Lori Kamola and Sharon Coan, editors, who saw value in our work. Thank you to Sara Johnson, Hillary Wolfe, and all members of the team who expertly and efficiently coordinated publication of this book. Lastly, a heartfelt thank you to Joan Irwin, our developmental editor, who meticulously organized enormous amounts of information, focused our thinking, and supported our vision. She provided the framework to move this guided reading practice from a pragmatic curriculum to a reflective consideration of the underlying literacy philosophies.

Introduction

Over 8 million students in grades 4–12 read below grade level, and 3,000 students with limited literacy skills drop out of high school every school day (NCTE 2006).

Middle school teachers are well aware of the issues underlying adolescent literacy development. Undoubtedly, these teachers, like us, are delighted to see the increased attention given to adolescent literacy from researchers, policy makers, and the public (Lee and Spratley 2010; NCTE 2006). These reports underscore concerns for the high adolescent dropout rate and the potential for a growing under-literate segment of society.

Working with adolescents in their classrooms, middle school teachers observe the characteristics of adolescents and the unique requirements of their learning as they grow towards literacy independence. These teachers will tell you that they were drawn to teaching in the middle grades because they love to tackle extreme challenges, and thoroughly enjoy the variety that comes with the ever-changing emotional, social, and intellectual changes that happen in any given student in any given hour. As we have taught adolescents, we have noticed a number of characteristics that play out each day in our classrooms. We have noticed that our students:

- have great imaginations and are very curious about the world
- love to be involved in their own learning
- can think about their thinking
- can reflect about what they learn
- like to argue when trying to persuade others to believe in their ideas

- really like to discuss their personal experiences (connections) with us

- crave attention from us even when they seem like they want us to go far away

- forget things easily

- like to test the acceptable classroom behaviors

- want to know that we truly care about them

- form long-lasting attitudes about reading and writing.

Literacy Needs of Adolescents

The most advanced parts of the brain do not complete their development until adolescence is over. A wild growth spurt happens to the prefrontal cortex during the adolescent years. This means that emotional control, impulse restraint, and the ability to make sound decisions are skills that are underdeveloped during the middle school years (Bradley 2003; Giedd 2007). Recent brain research reveals that adolescents are going through unprecedented physical, emotional, and intellectual changes. These changes are occurring in a very inconsistent, and sometimes backward-moving, manner. We cannot expect our students to learn a literacy concept and move smoothly on to the next, more involved concept. Rather, they are continually floating along, both up and down a continuum of reading strategies. To illustrate this point, think about the reading strategies of connecting, predicting, visualizing, questioning, inferring, and synthesizing. In a single guided reading discussion, an adolescent student may be able to connect to a character's actions because he has had the same experience. For instance, a student can connect to a character in the book because the character owns a dog. The student understands what it is like to take care of a dog because he also has a dog. In another chapter, the student may infer that a character's motivation to sell his pet is because the buyer owns a farm with a lot of land where the dog can run. However, the same student may struggle to predict the character's next action. Because of this erratic brain development, a student who may seem secure in a concept one day may inexplicably not be able to access the same concept the next day. The student's growth is not predictable. In short, adolescent literacy needs can be summed up in this way: *They need a lot of guidance some of the time and they need some guidance all of the time.* Figure 1 illustrates the variations in adolescent literacy progress.

Fig. 1. Conceptual Representation of Adolescent Literacy Progress

Given these facts about brain development during adolescence, it may seem nearly impossible to teach adolescents anything. However, as we have learned, middle school students have many strengths upon which to build. As we have developed these strategies for the guided reading approach to genre study, middle school students are most certainly capable of learning how to think deeply about text. That is the focus of this book.

Teachers agree that there are differences among students regarding how they learn. These differences are based on both individual learning preferences and individual student interests (Anderson 2007). This diversity in learning styles and interests, along with large differences in student ability levels, presents many challenges to middle school teachers when teaching adolescent readers. One challenge is finding different avenues to teach students to process and make sense of what they read. Another one is developing curricula and lessons so that all students within a classroom can learn effectively regardless of differences in their abilities. To address the diverse needs of students in your classes, draw upon the gradual release of responsibility model. In this model, the teacher leads the students through a process that begins with the teacher in full control of the learning and ends with student independence.

Our guided reading model reflects many of the characteristics of this gradual release of responsibility. Classes typically begin with a mini-lesson in which the concept or strategy is presented to the students; for example, symbolism in novels, or procedures for an effective discussion. This part of the process is teacher-led. The second stage involves modeling, and it occurs in the small group meeting. It is here that the concept is fleshed out and discussed and instruction is adjusted to meet the needs of a particular group of students. Student participation is much greater at this stage as the lesson is taught in a small group setting. Depending on the needs of students in the individual groups, the teacher input may be very short or a bit more involved. The guided practice stage occurs when the small group discusses specific questions or ideas that emerge from the text they are reading. In many ways this is the heart of the guided reading program, when the teacher works interdependently with the students. Make sure that there are ample opportunities to support student learning as needs arise, and

Stages of Gradual Release of Responsibility Model

- Teacher models a task or provides explicit information to the students.

- The task is shared between the teacher and students as a whole group.

- Students perform an activity or apply what they are learning with continued but reduced teacher support.

- Students practice independently as they move towards mastery.

(Pearson and Gallagher 1983)

that students are able to develop and demonstrate an understanding of the concepts being taught. When the students have been through these first three stages, they are ready for the final step in which they practice the concept or skill independently. Independent practice occurs throughout the year as the students apply what they have learned from previous group meetings and prepare for discussions about the text in a more independent manner. It takes time to this point, but when the students have reached this stage, they are able to direct the book discussions and the teacher's role morphs into that of a "silent observer."

These concepts that underpin the middle school guided reading model are rooted in research-based educational practices. Middle school language arts teachers know the goal is to develop strong readers who can comprehend a variety of texts with minimal assistance. But somewhere between the end of elementary school and the beginning of high school, some teachers stop emphasizing this effective approach to reading instruction—one that finds the just-right level of difficulty to enable each student to progress and flourish. The systematic and excellent practices of the elementary years—a balanced literacy approach that includes picture books, short and long fiction, and nonfiction sources, where small groups of students work with the teacher while other groups of students with similar abilities work with aides or parent volunteers—are slowly abandoned in middle school reading classes. Middle school typically features one large literature anthology and a couple of common novel studies throughout the year (Worthy, Moorman, and Turner 1999). The reading practices in place in elementary classrooms are more easily implemented in a flexible environment; however, the structured 40–50 minute middle school classes often result in more rigid teaching practices. Middle school reading instruction often begins and ends with unified whole-class discussions of texts where every student, regardless of ability, must read the same book at the same time in the same way. Sometimes the teacher reads aloud and the class follows along. Other times, the teacher plays a recording of the book while all students read along silently. Individual students may take turns reading aloud. Or, the students, as a group, can read the book silently.

There are disadvantages to each of these methods. The most obvious is the stress on students who cannot keep up. Even the most earnest adolescent will not learn to read at an optimal level simply by striving to follow a too-difficult text. Anyone who has struggled to read knows the feeling of dread waiting for your turn in the round-robin reading cycle to sound out words while the rest of the class snickers. Many students with lower fluency become discouraged by the pacing and give up. Meanwhile, highly fluent readers have to artificially slow their pace. Furthermore, these advanced students are not sufficiently challenged by the concepts, vocabulary, and sentence structures of the grade-level texts. Asking them to follow along with the rest of the class would be like asking a skilled sprinter to jog slowly around the track while the other runners catch their breath. It's not going to make them faster; it will just create frustration (Ivey 1999).

Middle grade teachers don't create these conditions because they are lazy, unimaginative, or ill-prepared. Many are responsible for teaching up to 150 students a day, sometimes multiple grade levels and subjects, while simultaneously dealing with 200–300 parents, grandparents, and various other guardians, maintaining acceptable test scores, and meeting the demands of administrators and district, state, and federal officials. They have limited time to reflect on best practices for teaching reading. In addition, few resources are available to show teachers how to effectively individualize reading instruction and assessment in the middle grades. The chart on the next page summarizes the challenges.

Challenges to Establishing Literacy Programs in the Middle Grades

Challenge	Description
Time	When the bell rings at the end of a typical 50-minute period, students leave for another class with a different teacher. The option of expanding time for reading instruction is rarely available.
Students	A middle school teacher may be responsible for up to 150 students a day. The responsibility for designing individualized reading instruction and assessment plans for every student can seem overwhelming.
Student Resources	Textbooks, anthologies, and novels for middle school students tend to be detailed, complex, and lengthy. Most literacy resources aimed at this age group require deeper thinking, vocabulary development, and reading strategies for deep comprehension.
Teacher Resources	Middle school reading resources often consist of a single large textbook, a grammar text, and a novel that the whole class must read together. These resources do not typically contain differentiated materials.

What You Will Find in This Book

Guiding Adolescent Readers to Success is designed to show you how to work within the common constraints of the middle school classroom and still achieve an effective literacy program that meets the needs of all your students. We call our approach *middle school guided reading*, which incorporates the best literacy practices from our training in elementary education and reflects the reality of our experience teaching in the middle grades. Even the best literacy practices of the elementary grades do not transfer seamlessly into the middle grades, just as the literacy practices used by high school teachers do not meet the needs of many middle school students. We have spent a number of years creating a hybrid of the most effective elementary literacy practices and shaping them to meet the comprehension needs of our adolescent learners. Teaching middle school is a carefully-planned and organized balancing act of addressing students' child-like behaviors while meeting their adult-like intellectual needs. After trying all sorts of traditional teaching practices employed in teaching literacy at the middle school level, we found that guided reading was the only method that addressed all the intellectual and social needs of adolescent students.

Some teachers feel that it is just too difficult to differentiate in a middle school. The program laid out here is based on very recent research and incorporates new concepts and ideas surrounding the development of the adolescent brain and it's specific needs. Much of these concepts and ideas are being updated as researchers gain knowledge of the adolescent brain. It would be nice if adolescents simply behaved like rationally miniature adults. However, they do not.

In previous years, it was customary to simply lecture to a class of adolescent students. When a principal observed a lesson, the teacher was often standing in front of the room lecturing while the students sat in straight rows taking notes. In this scenario, it would appear that the teacher was adequately transmitting material to the students. However, recent research regarding how people learn has proven this "transmission" model to be an ineffective way to teach. The guided reading program is embedded in a workshop model where students learn a new skill, practice this new skill in class, and articulate their acquisition of the skill in a guided reading meeting. It taps into all the learning needs of the adolescent student. While the adolescent student reads silently, it should not be assumed that he or she is not engaging in deep instructional practice. The student is enhancing his or her reading ability by applying the new skill—such as looking for a symbol in a piece of text—and then synthesizing the application of the skill by writing about what the symbol means. This activity strengthens the student's ability to use this reading strategy. When the student speaks up in a group, he or she is building analytical skills while thinking deeply about an author's use of symbolism, and while responding to the thoughts of another group member. Should a guest question the rigor of a guided reading classroom, a brief explanation from the teacher of what is happening or a direct question to a student will be sure to leave the visitor impressed.

Middle school guided reading consists of small group, text-based discussion meetings that serve as the vital part of a reader's workshop. The central focus of guided reading is the idea of coaching students toward a deeper understanding of fiction and nonfiction text while still allowing students to maintain a level of independence. In guided reading meetings, students are allowed to share their personal experiences and discuss the text in a more intimate setting. They may choose how much to read and when to meet again (within reason). They select their own vocabulary words to study and they always have a self-selected book to read in addition to a guided reading book. Guided reading provides opportunities for students to reflect and write about the literary focus or structural textual elements.

Even though students may roll their eyes in response to your requests, they really do crave individual attention. They love meeting with you in a guided reading session because they get a chance to talk about their reactions and connections to the text. This experience feeds into their emotional need to express their ideas and it helps you learn about their interests and use the knowledge to teach them to think deeply about literature. Always choose engaging young adult literature or high-interest nonfiction for your guided reading resources. Students enjoy reading something they are interested in. Although students are going through a lot of changes during this time, it is important to know that they are forming strong opinions about school. Guided reading provides an amazing opportunity to help them learn to love reading.

Guided Reading Meets Adolescents' Learning Needs

- Students select titles that reflect their interests
- Students help determine the amount of text to read
- Students are instructed in metacognition
- Teachers provide whole-class and small-group instruction for additional guidance
- Teachers use engaging questions about the text
- Students develop positive attitudes about literature

Teachers need to be able to assess students' needs. Considering that an adolescent's mind is in a state of growth and fluctuation, it makes sense to alter our teaching plans "in the moment" in order to address their intellectual spikes and valleys. Because guided reading involves small-group instruction, the student cannot hide in the back of the room as they might during a whole-group discussion. Consequently, the individual student's literacy needs can be addressed based on responses to your direct questions.

Fiction resources used in guided reading are selected by genre. In its most simple definition, a *genre* is like a category. Organize the books in categories—mystery, historical fiction, fantasy, science fiction, poetry—and plan instruction relevant to the characteristics of the genre. For example, in the science fiction genre, the setting will probably take place in an alternate universe or in space, and it will include a higher level of technology than we use in the present. By structuring guided reading units into genre studies, you can differentiate materials and instruction without losing the cohesiveness of the unit. For each genre, select three or four books at different reading levels. The reading levels are identified by Lexile scores (see Chapter 2). Try to select books at three levels of difficulty to accommodate the instructional needs of individual students. Begin each unit with a whole group mini-lesson that centers on the elements of the genre. The subsequent guided reading meetings allow for more specific instruction on reading strategies using specific events from the book, or further instruction about the characteristics of the genre. Each unit ends with a student activity, or reader's notebook entry, which provides questions to enable students to write and think more deeply about the text they have read. As you work with students in the small-group guided reading meetings, observe their progress and plan appropriate instruction. Furthermore, use a number of assessment tools to help learn more about your students as readers.

Overview of Chapters

Guiding Adolescent Readers to Success consists of nine chapters. The first eight chapters present foundational material about implementing the guided reading approach; the last chapter describes how to develop and use guided reading units.

Chapter 1: Achieving Reading Independence expands on the concepts of adolescent literacy development presented in the Introduction and shows how guided reading is effective in meeting the learning needs of these students.

Chapter 2: Getting Started with Guided Reading describes the features of guided reading in action, notably a 10-point plan for literacy success. Transcripts of teacher-student conversations illustrate the nature of learning activities in small-group meetings.

Chapter 3: Learning About Our Students as Readers describes assessment activities that can inform and shape instruction. Assessment data collected over time both from our classes and those of other teachers have demonstrated the effectiveness of guided reading on students' comprehension development.

Chapter 4: Fundamentals of Guided Reading delves into the practical realities of implementing guided reading with your students. We provide guidance about strategies for grouping, selecting books, and conducting guided reading meetings.

Chapter 5: Organizing for Guided Reading addresses critical questions about classroom management including silent reading time, student independence, scheduling time with each group, and building a collection of resources that serve student learning needs and interests. Examples of guided reading schedules for both teacher and students illustrate how class time can be used effectively.

Chapter 6: Enhancing Reading through Vocabulary Study and Writing describes strategies for building vocabulary and activities that involve students in writing in relation to the texts that they have read. These activities are designed to build students' comprehension of the texts.

Chapter 7: Establishing Reading Goals through Mini-lessons describes the features of mini-lessons and provides guidance for effective planning and use of such lessons. These lessons may focus on literary concepts, reading strategies, or procedures necessary for successful guided reading meetings. Remember that it is essential to be sensitive to the concept of *mini* in such lessons. If you're talking, the students aren't reading.

Chapter 8: The Impact of Guided Reading on Reading Comprehension Scores reveals the impact of this approach on students' reading performance, not only for our students but also for other teachers.

Chapter 9: Guidelines for Developing Guided Reading Units shows how you can create your own genre units based on this model. We provide information about the tasks involved in structuring the units, choosing books for the units, and differentiating instruction, as well as advice about keeping things in perspective.

Features of *Guiding Adolescent Readers to Success*

Because we are both practicing middle school teachers, we understand the joys and challenges that accompany teaching adolescents. We also know first-hand the many demands on teachers—planning lessons, assessing student progress, attending faculty meetings, communicating with students' parents/caregivers, all while attempting to maintain a productive personal life outside of school. Several features of this book are designed to invite you to think about your teaching in the context of this instructional model.

- In the Classroom with [Julie or Mark], at the beginning of each chapter, provides vignettes of our experiences as we planned lessons, interacted with our students, or reflected on what it means to be an effective teacher. We hope our stories help to convey the daily realities of teaching adolescents.

- Sidebars, interspersed throughout the chapters, include quotations relevant to chapter topics, as well as capsule statements of important concepts being described.

- Reflections on Adolescent Literacy, at the end of each chapter, offer questions that invite you to think about how you can draw on our experiences to create a literacy program that is satisfying to you and beneficial for your students. We hope that these suggestions and questions will inspire you and your colleagues to explore various avenues of teaching that will further the literacy development of your students and imbue them with a love of reading.

- Assessment Resources, shown in Appendix A, are examples of assessment tools and forms for recording data you can collect about your students.

- Student Comprehension Resources, shown in Appendix B, are examples of activity sheets you can reproduce for use in your own classroom.

- Examples of mini-lessons are included in Appendix C.

- Common Core State Standards for English Language Arts Grades 6–8 are presented in Appendix D.

- Guided Reading Unit Resources, used in our classrooms, are summarized in Appendix E.

- All references cited are detailed in Appendix F.

- Suggestions for Young Adult Literature to use during guided reading are listed in Appendix G.

- Suggestions for Young Adult Nonfiction to use during guided reading are listed in Appendix H.

- For more in-depth articles and resources on the topics addressed in this book, refer to the Recommended Reading listed in Appendix I.

Achieving Reading Independence

Chapter 1

In the Classroom with *Julie*

As a new teacher, I remember spending an entire week preparing my students to understand and be able to talk about the reading strategies of predicting and making inferences as these pertained to the novels they were studying. I was very excited about conducting the first literature circle meetings with my eighth grade students. Having felt that I had adequately taught them the strategies along with the rules of having a meaningful conversation about a book, I reminded them that I would be watching and listening and encouraged my students to stay focused. My students were grouped homogeneously with no more than eight students in each group. Their responsibilities were loose and flexible in order to allow for natural conversations to take place. I had modeled what a great literature circle looks like, and the students had practiced the routines.

As the six groups of students began talking quietly at the same time, the room buzzed with meaningful conversations—or did it? I wasn't sure. As I wandered around the classroom with my observation sheet, I heard snippets of conversations and glimpsed at the students' open reader's notebooks. I noticed that some students were sitting quietly, but because I hadn't participated in their groups I didn't know if they had already contributed to the conversation or were having trouble understanding. Other students did not have their written assignments completed, and I noted this. After 20 minutes, when I disbanded the groups, I had collected limited evidence of their deep understanding. I was too busy trying to attend to all groups within the meeting time.

My next attempt at conducting literature circles was to stagger the conversations by having only two groups meet each class period while the other students read silently. I found that I could more accurately assess students this way. But without being a member of the groups, I missed important teaching points. Furthermore, the silent readers were disturbed by the conversations of the discussion groups and as a result didn't get much done during that class period.

On my third attempt, I invited another teacher to help me observe my students and set up a video camera in the back of the classroom. This way, I could spend more time with each group and gather evidence and speak up when I thought I could move the conversation along. This approach worked well, but the other teacher was not always available to assist me and our observation strategies varied.

On several occasions, as I made my way to the group across the room, I overheard whispered conspiracies such as "here she comes," and the conversation took on an unnatural tone: "So, Joe, I really like what you said about the character." When I jumped in and responded with, "What exactly did Joe just say, and which character did he say it about?" the students could not reply. These students had been faking the interactions. I realized that I needed to be more of a presence with these students and try to figure out why this was happening.

I know that it's natural for students to get off-topic when they are in peer groups. It's also natural for an eighth grade group to try to fool the teacher. As I reflected on what I could have done to prepare them better, I realized that I needed to know more about them as readers. I fell back on my elementary education training and began to incorporate guided reading groups in my classes. By being an active part of the book conversation and taking on a coaching role in a guided reading session, I had the opportunity to assess my students' reading abilities in the moment and address the needs of both struggling readers and nonreaders. I could better engage the students who struggled with reading, by supporting their learning and providing them with information to fill in their comprehension gaps. For my students who chose to be nonreaders, I held them more accountable for their learning by sitting next to them and asking them direct questions. Guided reading meetings allowed me the opportunity to immediately intervene to prompt my students by asking them questions that led them to a deeper understanding of the text.

The Difference Between Guided Reading and Literature Circles

When Mark and I talk about the guided reading model, colleagues often assume that we are simply using a different term for literature circles. Other than the fact that all members of a group read the same text, there are significant differences between the two ways of organizing for reading practice. The most distinguishing factor is the teacher's role in increasing students' comprehension. In guided reading, the teacher is an active member of the group and prompts students to think deeply about the text through targeted questioning. Unlike the elementary model of guided reading, where there is a greater focus on students reading much shorter text with a higher level of teacher involvement, the middle school guided reading model emphasizes more independent learning appropriate to the adolescent's reading needs. By listening to student responses in the guided reading meeting, the middle school teacher can determine the need for follow-up mini-lessons about abstract literary concepts such as symbolism or point-of-view that will enable students to further probe the text. We have discovered that independent readers need to be monitored and guided just as carefully as those students who struggle with reading. Active intervention helps all students.

In literature circles, student autonomy is the focus—much like the guided reading model we propose—but with some differences. In this setting, the teacher typically spends time preparing the whole group to engage in meaningful conversations about text—helping students understand the roles and procedures for participating in the literature circle. The group is then released to conduct an independent discussion about the text and to reflect about what they've learned from the literature circle in a written format. This discussion is conducted in accordance with the teacher's mini-lesson, but student conversations often move independently.

Literature circles can provide an ideal setting for students to develop fluency and feel comfortable discussing important themes, vocabulary, and plot structures with peers at an approximately similar reading level. This approach is a big improvement on the practice of assigning every student the same texts and questions from the literature anthology.

However, many middle grade students —especially sixth graders—are not quite developmentally ready to participate in literature circles without regular and ongoing assistance from the teacher. These students need a more structured instructional setting that provides for gradual release to reading independently. They often require extensive preparation in the roles and procedures necessary to maintaining effective discussion in the literature circle, as well as instruction in reading strategies appropriate to the text being studied.

A challenge for teachers conducting literature circles is the difficulty of assessment. The teacher is primarily an outside observer and does not have consistent contact with students during book discussions. Consequently, the teacher may miss important clues about how well students comprehend the text or are able to apply effective reading strategies.

"Our experience suggests that teachers who are addressing the learning needs of all students employ a recursive instructional process that includes:

- Teacher modeling and guiding for the acquisition of new content

- Time for students to collaborate as they refine their understanding of new content

- Opportunities for students to try on the new content independently."

(Ross and Frey 2009)

Many of Julie's students needed the scaffolding that guided reading provided before she could release them to participate in the more independent tasks of literature circles. A summary of the different roles and responsibilities of teachers and students in traditional literature circles versus guided reading is shown here.

Comparing Roles and Responsibilities in Literature Circles and Guided Reading

Literature Circles	Guided Reading
Students... • all read the same text • develop fluency skills • focus on vocabulary, plot structures, and themes • respond to assigned questions and prompts • require extensive preparation in roles and procedures for independent work • must all read at the same pace to finish the book together	**Students...** • have choice in text selection within a genre • work in small groups with guidance from the teacher • focus on characteristics of genres, literary devices, and other elements to show evidence of deep understanding • can work at a pace that is optimal for their understanding
Teachers... • lead the group discussions • assign comprehension questions (often from an anthology) • focus on assessing fluency skills and basic comprehension	**Teachers...** • actively participate in discussions while gradually releasing responsibility to students • conduct follow-up mini-lessons as needed • assess use of specific comprehension strategies • provide text selections that are geared towards student interests • get to know their students as individual readers and learners

A Continuum of Reading Development

Ideally, all middle grade students should be able to conduct authentic and thoughtful conversations about the books they read. But in reality, they must move along a continuum. Guided reading groups in a middle school are fluid and change often, just as the dynamics of the group discussion and the teacher's involvement shift as needed. Figure 1.1 shows the continuum as students move towards the level of independence necessary to participate effectively in a literature circle.

Fig. 1.1. Moving Students Toward Independence

Guided Reading   Increased Student Responsibility   Literature Circles

Teacher leads small-group discussion	Teacher facilitates small-group discussion	Students lead small-group discussion

The concepts shown in figure 1.1 are consistent with the principles of the gradual release of responsibility model (see description in the Introduction). In the guided reading approach, the teacher has the ability to be flexible and easily move the students through the continuum from guided practice to shared instruction to independent practice, and, when appropriate, to move backwards along the continuum. Specifically, guided reading adds an important layer of flexibility that allows the teacher to adapt to the particular needs of a small group of students.

The middle school guided reading model lets students participate in small, focused conversations about books that are carefully selected for their needs and interests, a built-in form of differentiation. Teachers are deeply involved in the group meetings and guide the conversations. They may ask pointed questions when they want specific students to practice certain skills, or they may sit silently foremost of the meeting as the students discuss the text independently. Student autonomy is conditional and evolving, never static.

As the school year progresses, adjust the groups periodically to maximize student growth both academically and socially. Occasionally, some groups might be able to operate with significantly less direction than others. Maintain close ties with most groups through close observation, questioning, and direction.

Guided reading puts the teacher into the conversation on a much more personal level than either whole-group instruction or traditional literature circles. As Julie's experience shows, it is difficult to be responsive in the moment and to reflect on the nuances of students' reading needs when watching from afar. Guided reading provides the right degree of involvement for both teachers and students. One of the most powerful aspects of the guided reading experience is looking a student in the eye, asking a direct question, and knowing immediately if the student understands. The teacher can then make the decision, in the context of the small group, to re-teach, to broadly guide, or to simply observe. It is also in these moments that teachers who are responsible for 125–150 students every day can come to know their students as individual readers and learners.

"We now realize that peer-led reading groups need much more than a good launching; they require constant coaching and training by a very active teacher who uses mini-lessons and debriefing to help kids on skills like active listening, asking follow-up questions, disagreeing agreeably, dealing with 'slackers,' and more."

(Daniels 2006)

Genre Study within Fiction and Nonfiction

Organizing units in the guided reading model by genre creates a multi-dimensional, recursive learning environment. Framing units as genre studies provides students with explicit instruction in the elements of the selected genre so they know what to expect as they read and can use this knowledge to build meaning. Genre is considered to be an "overlooked cueing system," which provides a framework or road map for the students to follow as they search to find meaning as they read (Bomer 1995). Organizing instruction around genres provides an additional layer of support for students as they read and explore unfamiliar texts. The format works like this:

- Present some mini-lessons that focus on genre characteristics or text structures for nonfiction.

- In the guided reading groups, explore the characteristics in greater detail.

- Use insights from the guided reading sessions as talking points for the whole class during closing activities or remarks.

- Have students simultaneously read self-selected books within the genre.

- Include regular vocabulary study, drawn from the targeted books and the literature curriculum, to sharpen their skills.

- Ask students to write about assigned topics in their reader's notebooks—comparing the self-selected and guided reading group books, using new vocabulary, and reflecting on the reading strategies and themes introduced in mini-lessons.

- Check in with individual students to make needed adjustments.

It is certainly possible to teach a guided reading unit with books that are not linked by genre. Many young adult books have overlapping features emphasizing story elements or character development that can help students build strategic skills such as predicting and inferring. A robust unit can be developed with a diverse selection of books.

But genre studies have strong advantages. Chiefly, many state language arts standards require genre studies in the middle grades. Standards that do not require genre studies often direct teachers to use specific nonfiction categories such as personal narrative, informational text, persuasive text, and memoir for reading and writing activities. By organizing guided reading units around genres, you can teach the concepts as part of literature study and cycle back when specific writing assignments are developed at another time.

One of our middle school colleagues posed a fair question: "How in the world am I supposed to develop lesson plans for three or more books for every genre?" In the chapters that follow, we provide guidelines for creating guided reading units along with excerpts from some of the units we use with our students. We also provide examples of questions and techniques to ease record-keeping and grading. We hope you will add to these models as you gain greater confidence with guided reading and share your strategies and successes with colleagues.

Meeting the Needs of Adolescent Readers

In middle school, students encounter texts that feature language, structures, and concepts that may be far removed from the familiar literary and expository resources they had access to during their elementary school years. Increasingly, adolescent students interact with a wide variety of texts in both print and non-print forms—popular and classical literature, nonfiction including content-area texts, magazines, music, websites, and video clips. In all these experiences, students have opportunities to make connections between their personal lives and the external worlds of school and society. An effective middle school literacy program capitalizes on this range of experience by providing activities that nurture and extend student interests, their repertoire of reading strategies, their appreciation of different genres, and their capacity to express themselves in both oral and written forms. Such activities, including frequent opportunities for students to select their own reading materials, facilitate their progress toward literacy independence. As we developed the guided reading program, we were sensitive to the needs of our students, but we also knew that the program had to incorporate sound practices supported by research. Features of our guided reading program and relevant research findings about what adolescent readers need are summarized in the chart below.

Guided Reading Aligns with Literacy Research

Research indicates...	Guided reading provides...
The process of explicit instruction follows a pattern typified by direct explanation of the strategy, teaching modeling, guided practice, and application within a context that encourages students to learn how to monitor and regulate their reading behavior (RAND 2002; Biancarosa and Snow 2004).	Explicit instruction in comprehension strategies, vocabulary, and genre characteristics.
Adolescent readers need "sustained experiences with diverse texts in a variety of genres and offering multiple perspectives on real life experiences" (NCTE 2004). "...adolescent students who participate in programs that connect literacy with real-life out-of-school issues and personal interests indicate more positive feelings about reading and writing in school" (Ivey and Broaddus 2001).	A variety of genres, including science fiction, mystery, poetry, historical fiction, and adventure, and nonfiction categories such as biography, persuasive text, or essays. In a guided middle school classroom, there may be as many as four different titles being used for teacher-led instruction and 30 additional titles being read by individual students.
"Differentiated instruction helps students not only master content, but also form their own identities as learners" (Tomlinson 2008). Motivation and self-directed learning are supported in a classroom environment that provides resources and instructional activities that accommodate individual learning needs (Biancarosa and Snow 2004).	Materials within individual genres that represent various levels of reading difficulty so that instruction can be differentiated to meet student needs.

Guided Reading Aligns with Literacy Research *(cont.)*

Research indicates...	Guided reading provides...
Adolescent learners need "conversations/ discussions regarding texts that are authentic, student initiated, and teacher facilitated. Such discussion should lead to diverse interpretations of a text that deepens the conversation" (NCTE 2004). Text-based collaborative learning enables students to learn by interacting with one another around a variety of texts (Biancarosa and Snow 2004).	Small group sessions—guided reading meetings—in which the teacher and students engage in discussions intended to deepen comprehension and build interpersonal communication skills.
"Many texts must be read in common by an entire class, as the curriculum dictates, but allowing some discretion for students to choose their own texts increases motivation, especially because these selections can help students make connections between the texts and their own worlds. Of course, reading self-selected texts also increases reading fluency, or the ability to read quickly and accurately" (NCTE 2006).	Opportunities for students to self-select materials for independent reading and time for students to read these texts.
"Writing can help students understand, process, and think critically about course material. Writing assignments, then, are best designed to help students learn: by asking them first to use writing to learn about a given topic or subject, to evaluate their own understanding of that topic, and/or to develop expertise about it; then to use writing to critically analyze that understanding" (NCTE 2008).	Writing activities designed to foster student reflection.
Ongoing formative assessment guides the teacher's planning for instruction and helps students recognize strengths and challenges in their learning (Biancarosa and Snow 2004).	Embedded assessment routines in guided reading meetings, mini-lessons, and writer's reflections about the text studied.

Many aspects contribute to an effective adolescent reading program. This guided reading approach contains the necessary ingredients for students to achieve reading independence. In the chapters that follow we provide details that will enable you to implement guided reading in your own classroom.

Reflections on Adolescent Literacy

Read the following quotations. Then answer the questions below.

"When students are not recognized for bringing valuable, multiple-literacy practices to school, they can become resistant to school-based literacy" (NCTE 2007).

"Adolescents may struggle with text for a number of reasons, including problems with

- vocabulary knowledge
- general knowledge of topics and text structures
- knowing of what to do when comprehension breaks down
- proficiency in monitoring their own comprehension."

(Lee and Spratley 2010)

1. In what ways do these quotations reflect what you have experienced in teaching adolescents? Share your reactions to these quotations with colleagues.

2. Based on your reading of the Introduction and Chapter 1, what are your initial reactions to the guided reading model the authors advocate? In what ways can you see the potential for implementing guided reading in your classroom?

Getting Started with Guided Reading

Chapter 2

In the Classroom with Mark

The first morning bell rings and students begin sauntering through the classroom door, busily chatting about their experiences on Facebook or the latest video they viewed on YouTube™. By the time the last bell signals, all of the eighth graders are at their desks with books in hand. Gus is quickly lost in the book, *A Boy No More* (Mazer 2006), following the World War II story about a child's torn loyalty between a father killed at Pearl Harbor and a Japanese-American friend. Jonathan sits nearby, reading *Chains* (Anderson 2008), a novel that a teacher had recommended about a slave trapped in New York City during the Revolutionary War. At her desk, Maddie is quickly scratching out the answers to the questions generated during her guided reading group meeting a few days before. She wants to have her responses prepared for tomorrow's gathering.

Across the classroom, Shelby writes in her reader's notebook. Based on the mini-lesson from yesterday, she analyzes the way Laurie Halse Anderson, author of *Chains*, develops the theme of independence through the main character's deepening personality traits. Meanwhile, James browses the classroom library. He has had trouble remembering to bring his self-selected reading to class. As he flips through the multitude of books available, he is glad to find one that looks interesting and not too tough. He returns to his seat.

Off in a corner of the classroom, I huddle with six students who have arranged their chairs in a semi-circle. They speak quietly but passionately about the text, *Elijah of Buxton* (Curtis 2009), a book they have been reading together.

"I don't think Elijah should have been hit," Vanessa says about the main character in *Elijah of Buxton*. "What he said was awful and racist, but it really didn't call for being smacked across his face so hard that he fell to the ground."

In my role as facilitator, I respond with a follow-up question to encourage the students to reflect on Vanessa's insight. Additionally, I observe that one student has not participated in the discussion so far; I make a note to check in with the student later to assess his comprehension and engagement.

Mark: (*speaking to Vanessa*) What does this action tell you about Mr. Leroy?

Vanessa: It tells me he's mean.

Tonja: (*picking up the conversation strand*) Well, I think Mr. Leroy is harsh, but he hit Elijah for a reason. He was teaching him a lesson.

Vanessa: (*making a personal connection*) That's no way to teach a lesson. I'd be real mad if someone hit me for that.

Mark: (*redirecting the group back to the second student's comment*) Tonja, you said Mr. Leroy had a good reason for hitting Elijah. Help us understand what you mean. Why do you think Mr. Leroy had a good reason to do what he did?

For the next five minutes, the group continues analyzing the characters' actions and motivations. As both observer and participant in the guided reading conversation, I get a more nuanced view of the group's progress. The students understand how a single word, *nigg-,*[sic] the one Elijah used, can convey prejudice against an entire race of people, but I realize that I will need to extend the students' thinking by prompting them to consider Elijah as a symbol of emerging freedom for slaves.

As the members of this guided reading group return to their seats, I gather another group for a meeting about *Code Talker* (Bruchac 2005) to discuss the irony present in the story. Ten minutes later, the second group disperses and I call the whole class together for a sharing session to wrap up the reading talks.

Mark: We learned that an author will use the actions of characters to teach a lesson about human nature or life. This is called the *theme* of the story. Who can tell me about the theme of their self-selected text and explain how your character's actions illustrate this theme? Remember, support your thinking by telling us what specifically happened in the book that gave you an insight into the theme.

Dave: I think Elijah is a pretty funny kid who gets along with his parents. There was a part in the beginning of the book where Elijah played a trick on his mom and put a toad in her sewing basket, knowing that she was afraid of toads. His mom jumps up in surprise and runs into the house. Elijah and his dad try to cover up their laughter but his mom hears them. She ends up getting back at him by playing an even bigger trick on him by placing a live snake in a cookie jar! As Elijah reached in to get a 'rope' cookie, he grabbed the snake and was so scared that he ran a mile down the road with it still in his hand! I think the theme here is family love and the sense of community. The author, Christopher Paul Curtis, shows us how much Elijah and his family 'play' together and love each other in this part. They seem to be a really tight family.

I observe that the image Dave has described elicits excited connections from other students.

Sara: Yeah, Christopher Paul Curtis always makes good characters that make you laugh. I think Elijah has a great relationship with his parents, and this book should be funny like another book I'm reading called *The Watsons Go to Birmingham—1963* (Curtis 1995).

Mai: Oh yeah! I read that one too, and it is super funny! The family in that book is very close, too. I think Christopher Paul Curtis writes funny stories about real things that happen to real families. It reminds me of my own family and the goofy stuff that happens to us. I think a theme in *Watsons...* is about close family relationships, too.

The bell rings, signaling the end of the period, and the students rush out of the classroom to get back to their hallway dramas. Another group of students enters and the guided reading dynamics begin again.

Reading Classes that Are Rigorous and Fun

To the untrained eye, the previous discussions may seem little more than casual conversations about books. But the dialogue reveals rich learning orchestrated by conscientious teaching in concert with the guided reading model. As the centerpiece of literacy instruction, guided reading gives teachers the ability to thoughtfully choose probing questions and prompts to assess students' understanding in the moment. Additionally, insights from the guided reading discussions help teachers reinforce a mini-lesson that might have started the class, as well as identify misconceptions that must be cleared up by the end of the period.

Prior to the discussions with students described in the previous vignette, Mark started the class by teaching a mini-lesson on the use of themes in novels, comparing them to an author's message about human nature. After setting this context, Mark used each of the scheduled guided reading meetings to link the book's themes to the main characters' actions. Through specific questions and prompts to guide students' verbal and written responses, he could then differentiate his instruction—providing more practice time for some students, adding a layer of complexity for others, and building interest for all students with texts at the appropriate reading levels. A brief wrap-up brought the whole class back to the purpose of the day's lesson before the period ended.

Each of the key components of the guided reading model will be discussed in greater detail in upcoming chapters. Here we just want to set the stage for success in getting started with guided reading. The chart on the next page shows the format and underscores the specific support that each component offers to middle school students.

Guided Reading in Action: A 10-point Plan for Literacy Success

Components of Guided Reading	Support of Student Understanding
Ongoing assessment of learning	The teacher conducts individual assessments of students to determine their reading levels and to place them in appropriate small groups. Formative and summative assessments from reading groups, assignments, and individual book talks enable the teacher to move students as needed throughout the year.
Selecting books for guided reading groups	The teacher provides a diversity of quality reading materials to motivate students to read.
Mini-lessons	Through an overview of a specific reading strategy or a literary topic, the teacher provides the context and purpose of each unit. Exploring these concepts with small groups and in whole-class sessions also gives students time to listen, practice, and reflect on new information.
Conducting small-group meetings	Students receive direct comprehension assistance from the teacher and reinforcement from peers. The teacher assumes dual roles as participant and observer. Acting in these roles enables the teacher to build relationships with students, discuss effective reading strategies, provide immediate feedback, probe and prompt thinking, and gather formative assessment data to refine and adjust instruction.

Guided Reading in Action: A 10-point Plan for Literacy Success *(cont.)*

Components of Guided Reading	Support of Student Understanding
Self-selected texts	Students choose their own texts, apply effective reading strategies, and develop the habit of reading independently.
Reader's reflections	Students keep a reader's notebook where they respond to questions that reinforce writing objectives as well as their thinking about the text.
Vocabulary study	Students acquire new words through reading and focused vocabulary study.
Whole-class discussions	Students share their thinking about the text during whole-class discussions. The dialogue reinforces common themes and lets groups learn about each other's books, which can generate interest in books for independent reading.
Effective classroom management strategies	Students learn and practice appropriate behavior while working independently and in groups. Because students always have something "to do," they feel purposeful and have fewer opportunities to get into trouble.
One-to-one discussions	These discussions give the teacher the opportunity to provide individual feedback to students.

Ongoing Assessment of Learning

Many activities occur in the guided reading classroom. Getting a guided reading program off the ground requires a conscious melding of effective classroom management procedures and timely mini-lessons to prepare the students for what is to come in the unit. But good assessment provides the foundation for starting and maintaining an effective guided reading program.

The initial reading assessment, the biggest undertaking of the year, determines student placement in the guided reading groups. However, you will continually monitor students' progress, adapt instruction, and adjust the reading groups throughout the year based on other formal and informal evaluations. Chapter 3 provides more details about effective assessment tools and responses; in Appendix A you will find a selection of assessment resources.

As soon as possible in the new term, you will want to evaluate each student's reading skills to determine:

- **Comprehension.** Can the student read actively and purposefully, interpreting the meaning of selected texts?

- **Vocabulary.** Does the student recognize and understand words and terminology that are appropriate for the designated grade level?

To become a fully functioning, self-actualized person, each young adolescent should:

- Be able to think rationally and critically and express thoughts clearly.

- Read deeply to independently gather, assess, and interpret information from a variety of sources and read avidly for enjoyment and lifelong learning.

- Develop the interpersonal and social skills needed to learn, work, and play with others harmoniously and confidently.

(National Middle School Association 2010)

- **Application of reading strategies.** Can the student do more than just decode words and explain the literal meaning of the text? Can the student also visualize a scene, make predictions based on prior reading, and synthesize ideas from a variety of texts?

- **Fluency.** How quickly and accurately can the student read a selection of grade-level text?

Selecting Books for Guided Reading Groups

One of the many benefits of guided reading is the autonomy involved in choosing books for students to read in their groups. We frame our book choices under the umbrella of the genre study and then analyze potential books for the concepts that reinforce our state standards. Our focus is on the comprehension skills and literary devices students need to learn at each specific grade level, including nonfiction that supports specific text structures as well. Although selecting engaging books is important, the real focus is the suitability of the books to meet the literacy needs of the students. Of course, you should choose books that are both engaging and appropriate for student needs.

The baseline reading assessment for each student will help you, to some extent, narrow the list of books. Be careful to avoid simply selecting books based on their designated grade level. Choose books based on your students' literacy needs and personal interests.

The Lexile Framework® for Reading scale, which represents the difficulty of a text, can further help refine your search for appropriate books (MetaMetrics 2007). The search engine at www.Lexile.com lets you sort books using titles, authors' names, keywords, and Lexile ranges. Lexiles focus primarily on sentence length and complexity and vocabulary. It does not factor in the content of the book or the complexity of a plot, which can make seemingly simple stories much more difficult to comprehend. The Lexile Framework is useful, but should not be the only factor you consider in choosing a book.

The overall quality of the book is another factor to take into account. Some young adult books are entertaining, but are not sufficiently robust for instructional purposes. These books might be suitable for the students' self-selected reading, but to maximize the time spent in guided reading group sessions, look for such well-regarded books as Newbery Honor winners or the Coretta Scott King award winners.

The content of the book is another important factor to consider based on the culture of the school and community. Advanced readers might be capable of reading and understanding certain texts, but that doesn't mean they are mature enough to handle the content. The definition of *appropriate* varies from family to family and from school to school. Be aware of and sensitive to the community's standards. (Lists of award-winning books for adolescent readers are available at the The American Library Association's website, http://www.ala.org.)

Finally, be mindful of students' interests. While the guided reading groups don't offer students the same choices as the self-selected reading, you can still select books that will engage and challenge them. When students are motivated to read a book, they will often surpass the expectations suggested by comprehension and vocabulary levels. The higher the interest you can generate, the better. Look for books that represent a diversity of gender, race, ethnic and socioeconomic groups in positive ways.

"The reading of literature invites students in an important conversation. Literature, and we include in that category the excellent literature for children and young adults, addresses the interesting and eternal questions about human experience. It asks readers to think about what they value, what they reject, what they accept, and what they would fight for."

(Beers and Probst 2011)

Mini-lessons

Mini-lessons are short (usually about 10 minutes), focused lessons designed to support student learning. Although a liberal dose of mini-lessons is good medicine for guided reading, you won't want to use these lessons every day because they would eat into the time for group sessions and independent reading.

You can use mini-lessons to explore effective reading strategies, discuss the rules of the reader's workshop sessions, and teach students how to listen to each other's responses to literature. This time is well spent because it establishes the framework for guided reading and the conditions for optimum learning. (For examples of mini-lessons, see Chapter 7.)

Mini-lessons can also be modified and retaught to a particular reading group as needed. These reinforcements serve to remind students about the main ideas of a mini-lesson taught earlier in the week or to refresh a concept taught earlier in the year.

Teachers often ask, "How do I know which mini-lesson to teach?" Consider your students' needs and your curricular objectives and standards. Mini-lessons are like links in a chain. They help students stretch from the starting point to the goal.

Guided Small-group Meetings

Differentiated groups are the key to the guided reading model. These groups usually consist of four to six students (or fewer if assessment shows that some students need more assistance). Based on our experience, we strongly recommend that no more than six students be included in the group. Having more than six students in the group makes it difficult to facilitate the conversation and to keep the meeting focused and on schedule.

In the guided reading groups, the students read the same book individually, focusing on skills, strategies, or themes that the teacher assigns in the guided reading meeting. These focus questions are based on the students' reading comprehension needs. Another option may be for the teacher to assign a focus question to reinforce the whole group mini-lesson. When students are finished reading and writing in response to their reading, they return to the group to discuss these ideas.

Students usually have two to four days between guided reading meetings, which should be sufficient time to complete the assignments. As the teacher, your involvement can vary widely from group to group depending upon the time of year, the developmental needs of the students, and the challenges of a particular book. Sometimes you may find yourself being directive within a guided reading meeting, while at other times, you will be facilitating the discussion. You should be comfortable with the idea that guided reading groups are dynamic and members of each group will change throughout the year.

To understand just how different your role can be in a guided reading gathering and to illustrate that not all lessons go as planned, consider the following conversations from two of Mark's groups that were reading *A Wrinkle in Time* (L'Engle 1962). Mark differentiated his instruction by choosing a different focus area for each group. The examples are excerpts from the discussions Mark had with different groups of students.

Mark: The last time we met, we learned about symbolism. I asked you to focus on "the black thing". What do you think the black thing stands for in this story?

Omar: I think the black thing is a black cloud that comes over the planet.

Mark: It does appear to float over the planet. But what could it stand for? What is it symbolic of? Remember how we used the American flag as a symbol and said it represented freedom but it wasn't *actually* freedom, and could not give you instant freedom? It is a symbol that stands for something else. We said that if I gave you the flag to hold in your hand, you would not be able to run around the school doing anything you like because you held freedom in your hand. Right?

Omar: Right! I couldn't walk out of the school or run through the halls and have two lunches.

Lin: Oh, so "the black thing" is like the American flag?

Mark: Sort of. The black thing represents something else just like the American flag represents freedom. What could the black thing represent in this story? I'll give you a hint: think about the color black and what you already know about characters in movies who wear black.

Lin: (*interrupts*) Oh, I know. I think it means something bad will happen during the night.

Omar: It will destroy the planet—just like Darth Vader in *Star Wars*.

Mark: Yes, much like Darth Vader, the black thing represents evil. This black thing will devour the planet if people don't fight it and stand up for love. In our next meeting, you will read about IT. IT is the name of the controller of the black thing. As you read further, think about why Madeleine L'Engle chose to name the bad person in the book IT, and not a real name like Joe.

This meeting was not what Mark expected and he had to take on a more explicitly directive role. The conversation was somewhat unnatural and did not flow as one would expect in a book club. However, the meeting provided useful formative assessment—these students did not fully understand symbolism—which showed Mark that he had to reteach an important literary concept. In a whole-group setting, he might have missed this gap in comprehension.

Many variables play a part in how well students will converse in any given meeting. For example, the time of the meetings can be a factor. In meetings scheduled right after lunch, students may either be very active or lethargic. In the former case, you will have to work hard to manage the conversations so that each member gets a chance to speak. In the other case, the meeting can be like "pulling teeth" from the group members—depending on what they ate for lunch and how hot it was outside that day. Mark knew that he had to reteach the concept of symbolism in a different way to two of the students in that group. Later, he used the silent reading time to engage each of those students in a one-to-one conversation to clarify the concept.

Now let's take a look at an excerpt from a second group.

> **Mark:** In our last meeting, Connie mentioned that the black thing symbolized the oppression of the human race and the evil that is inside every one of us. What message do you think Madeleine L'Engle was trying to convey when she chose to name the evil brain, "IT"?

> **Katie:** I found that she didn't give it a real name because she may have thought it did not deserve a real name. She named it a pronoun as to say that it wasn't worthy of a name.

> **Connie:** I disagree. I think she named it "IT" to symbolize that it could be anything and everything. Pronouns stand for a person, place, or thing right? By naming the evil thing "IT", with all capitals, she is stressing that its power can come from all negative things.

This meeting continued in a productive way and exceeded Mark's goals. In fact, he did not plan for this particular conversation but was delighted to see how the students were synthesizing what they read and connecting the text to their own lives. Furthermore, later in the discussion they referenced a previous guided reading book that contained descriptions of the evil acts of the Khmer Rouge. This conversation is an example of what we strive for in all of our guided reading groups.

We realize that many factors, such as "stop everything and test" mandates from the state and finding appropriate reading assessment tools, may affect how soon you can set up your ideal guided reading groups. Don't let these distractions discourage you from adopting informal gatherings of readers in the meantime.

You can have guided reading groups running well by early October or sometimes as late as mid-November. During the first six to eight weeks of the school year, while assessing students individually, also teach and reinforce your expectations for assignments and behavior. Teachers need to know the interests and qualities of their students as intimately as good novelists understand their characters. Strong relationships fuel learning. What students like and dislike, how they perceive the world, and who inspires them—these answers are key to unlocking the minds of young adolescents (Rog and Kropp 2001).

Guided reading groups create opportunities to get to know students better. Yes, the meetings provide an abundance of assessment data that you can mine throughout the year. But the personal revelations are just as important. The quicker you can get students into the habit of reading, discussing, and writing about developmentally appropriate books, the faster your relationship-building project will proceed.

Independent Reading of Self-selected Texts

The purpose of self-selected texts is to foster the love of reading and establish a culture of readers within your classroom. Students enjoy free reading time and place a higher value on it than any other language arts activity (Ivey and Broaddus 2001). Research also shows that students who read for a substantial amount of time, with 45 minutes being the optimal, show considerable increases in reading comprehension (Allington 2001). The evidence strongly supports the belief that students who read more are better readers. There is also evidence that reading contributes to higher achievement and does not merely correlate with it (Allington 2001).

Require students to keep track of the books they read so you can use the information when reviewing the materials and conferring with them. If you notice that a student is reading nothing but fantasy novels, for example, you might suggest a book that reaches outside their favorite genre. Continually monitor what the students are reading by talking to them and prompting them to explore stories that are beyond their current interests.

For instance, Julie noticed that a student had read almost every book in the *Harry Potter* series and claimed to only like "fantasy" books. She introduced him to *Touching Spirit Bear* (Mikaelsen 2001), a wonderful adventure story whose main character is a young boy about the same age as Harry Potter. Although there is no magic mentioned in the second novel, the books share a common theme of inner discipline that the main character had to master in order to achieve his goals. The student who read and enjoyed *Touching Spirit Bear* later acknowledged that he didn't think he would like adventure novels at all. His next book choice was an action novel called *Silverfin* (Higson 2009). Julie realized that what the student valued most was a book whose main character was a boy; the specific genre proved incidental to his interests. Based on this information, Julie could refer the student to a range of appealing books. By the end of the school year, he had read books from action, adventure, realistic fiction, biography, historical fiction, and fantasy genres.

By taking a few moments to talk to each student about his or her reading choices, you can help each one choose the next book as well as discuss why a current selection may be a struggle. These short conversations not only help broaden students' reading tastes, but they also help the teacher connect to the students and learn what motivates them to read.

Some parents express concern about their children reading two books at one time. Independent reading reinforces the genre study and gets students in the habit of reading widely and independently. Discourage students from taking the guided reading books out of the classroom unless there is a particular need; for example, that they have been absent for a number days, they have fallen behind on their reading, or they have a pending absence. Provide 30–40 minutes of reading time for each student on most days and schedule guided reading meetings far enough apart so that even the slower readers have time to read and be prepared for their meetings. If other members of the guided reading group finish the assigned guided reading sections ahead of time, ask that they set aside the guided reading books and read their self-selected books. This helps manage differences in students' fluency and discourages quick readers from reading too far ahead. It also keeps the classroom very quiet. Students should always have something to read or write about.

Reader's Reflections

Each school year, we promise parents that their children will read and write in class almost every day. Within every guided reading unit, students are continually reflecting on the text. The use of the reader's notebook encourages students to come to the guided reading meetings with prepared, thoughtful responses. When students are reluctant to speak within the group, you can always ask them, "What did you write down?"

The reader's notebook entries also provide additional insights into student thinking. By occasionally collecting and reviewing the student work or by quickly looking at a response during a guided reading meeting, you can assess whether students understood the question or if they missed the point. An incomplete notebook also can indicate that a student is struggling to complete the reading assignments. This could be because the reading is too difficult or it could be because the student is not motivated to complete the work. Whatever the reason, you can search for an appropriate and timely intervention.

The reader's notebook, a written response journal, is an artifact that illustrates the convergence of a number of state and national standards, including reading and building an understanding of diverse texts from a genre, applying reading strategies, demonstrating note-taking skills, using writing to communicate ideas, and participating as knowledgeable and critical members of a learning community.

Although mastery of the curriculum remains the driving force behind best teaching practices, you are required to assign letter grades for assignments. The students' reader's notebooks provide tangible evidence, in addition to embedded assessments, on which to base a grade.

Vocabulary Study

As students read, they are also learning new vocabulary words, and we want to show them how to decipher and analyze unfamiliar words and phrases. Support this authentic vocabulary building by explicitly teaching them how to use context clues correctly along with direct instruction of roots, suffixes, and prefixes. Our approach to vocabulary study uses both direct instruction and incidental learning. *Incidental learning* is learning that happens through the exposure to and interaction with increasingly complex and rich oral language and by encountering a lot of new words in texts through reading (National Reading Panel 2000).

To support this process, for each reading selection, students select vocabulary words that they would like to explore further. The goal is to generate a repository of words that will be displayed on the word wall (Cunningham and Allington 1994). Add words to the word wall as students encounter them in their shared reading and study of individual words (Allen 2007). Explain the criteria and practice defining and evaluating word wall words at the beginning of the school year, then refine the skills as you go along.

Whole-class Discussions

Routine and extended whole-class discussions of books can cause many students to mentally check out and many conversations to become didactic. But short sharing sessions, often coming at the end of class when you are wrapping up the day's guided reading groups and independent work, encourage students to learn from each other and build the classroom community. Effective prompts, such as extending themes from the guided reading group discussions, are essential. Instead of seeming like just another dry discourse on literacy analysis, the questions can become invitational, intriguing, and inspiring. Summarizing and expanding on specific students' comments shows them that you have paid attention to their insights and value their contributions.

Effective Classroom Management Strategies

In order to teach successfully using the guided reading model in the middle school, it is essential that classroom management be focused and effective. To allow students to focus on independent reading while other students are in a small group discussion requires that all students be doing what is required of them at the appropriate time. Students have to be aware of the classroom routines and your expectations for their behavior in whole-class, small group, and independent activities. Because such routines don't develop overnight, it is important to use mini-lessons to establish the guidelines for classroom routines—specific and focused work helps to maintain a classroom culture that is conducive to middle school guided reading. Specifics for classroom management are explained in Chapter 5.

One-to-One Discussions

One of the most enjoyable and informative aspects of the guided reading classroom is the opportunity to interact with students individually through quick conversations about the books they are reading. These informal and spontaneous meetings should always be part of the teaching protocol. Because of the tremendous amount of social pressure to appear just like everyone else, adolescents don't like to admit when they are having trouble comprehending. Private consultations give them a secure place to reveal challenges without embarrassment. The following transcript reveals a conversation Julie had with a seventh grade student during silent reading time.

Julie: Hey Marina, what are you reading?

Marina: *Defining Dulcie* by Paul Acampora (2006).

Julie: It's been a long time since I read that one. Would you remind me?

Marina: It's about a girl named Dulcie. Her dad died because he accidentally mixed ammonia and bleach in a cleaning solution. He was a custodian in a school.

That comment showed that Marina had some grasp of the plot, but Julie recalled that Marina often struggled to move past a superficial understanding of the storyline. Much of Marina's understanding came from her ability to make emotional connections with characters, so Julie decided to build on that strength.

Julie: That sounds pretty sad. What do you think about this story so far?

Marina: (*frowning*) I'm a bit confused. It's like, Dulcie's dad just died and she makes fun of it. Who would do such a thing? In the beginning of the book, she pretends that his death was a movie scene, and she even names the actor who would be her dad in the movie! I'm having a hard time getting into this story because I can't imagine anyone acting this way.

Julie: I think people grieve in different ways. I know when I'm really sad, I make jokes to cover up the pain I'm feeling. I think that's what Dulcie is doing. Don't give up on this story just yet; read on and give Dulcie a chance.

From this interaction, Julie learned that Marina was using her ability to make strong connections to characters to support her comprehension. However, Julie also recognized that Marina needed additional coaching about inference, so she made a note to conduct a mini-lesson about this topic within the next few days. Several other students were struggling with this concept, so reinforcement was necessary. Julie realized that Marina was thinking about abandoning the self-selected text. She decided to encourage Marina to stay with the book because it seemed to be providing good opportunity for growth.

Meeting the Standards

Another positive feature of the guided reading model is its adaptability in addressing academic standards. There are literally dozens of sets of standards, both state and national. Most of these standards fall under similar broad concepts regarding the use of reading strategies and the understanding of literary concepts. Whatever standards you need to follow, and however they are termed, the guided reading lessons can be tweaked to meet the requirements of the district or state standards. You'll find that this guided reading model supports the Common Core Curriculum Standards particularly well, since these standards require students to understand the craft and structure of text, and to integrate knowledge and ideas (Common Core State Standards Initiative 2010).

Putting the Components into Place

As you step back and consider all the components of the guided reading program, keep in mind that they represent what good teachers do almost instinctively:

- look for opportunities to differentiate instruction and assessment so all students can grow

- make notes, mental or otherwise, of what students need to do to get better

- put interesting books in the hands of students

- facilitate engaging conversations around the texts.

This guided reading model is not complicated. It simply creates a research-based system for providing individualized instruction, which helps deal with the challenges of modern middle schools. The best way to reach young adolescents is to know them well. Although this process continues throughout the school year, it starts with an initial assessment of their reading skills that we will discuss in Chapter 3.

Guided reading in middle schools draws together the effective reading strategies that, for years, researchers have been advocating and teachers have been applying. This approach simply takes these well-used strategies and establishes a framework that adapts them for the adolescent learner and fits them into the time constraints of a typical middle school schedule. The details in the following chapters are meant to provide a road map to help today's middle school teachers meet the ever-increasing demands placed upon them, their students, and their schools.

Reflections on Adolescent Literacy

Read the quote below and then answer the questions that follow.

"Adolescence is an era of tremendous personal and cognitive growth with some similarities to, but also differences from, the years before and after. New skills and strategies are needed to do well as the school years progress and student needs, interests, and abilities shift" (Langer 2009).

1. In what ways does the guided reading model described in this chapter reflect the ideas expressed in this quotation?

2. Which aspects of the guided reading model reflect what you already do in your middle school classroom?

3. To what extent do the transcripts of Julie's and Mark's conversations with students reflect what happens in your classroom?

Learning About Our Students as Readers

In the Classroom with *Julie*

When I first began teaching in a middle school, it was customary to assign one novel to an entire class. This approach included a lot of whole-group instruction about reading assignments given as homework. The conversation that follows is representative of many that took place in my classroom at that time.

Julie: Good morning, students. You read the first three chapters of *The Outsiders* (Hinton 1997) last night for homework. Who can explain who the Greasers are?

Sophie: They are the gang that Ponyboy belongs to. He describes them as his family because his brothers are in the gang. They have long hair and they grease it back. They get into trouble a lot. They are considered to be "tuff."

Julie: Fantastic! Why is belonging in the gang important to Johnny, Ponyboy's best friend?

Tyrone: Johnny had an awful family life. His mom and dad treat him badly. The Greasers are like his family.

Julie: How does Ponyboy's relationship with Darry differ from his relationship with Sodapop?

Dominique: Ponyboy is much closer to Sodapop than he is to Darry. He doesn't like the way Darry treats him. He thinks Darry is mean and unfair.

Peter: (*raising his hand*) I think Ponyboy is too immature to think about the pressure Darry is under. I mean, he is raising the family. He wants Ponyboy to do well and stay out of trouble.

Dominique: I think Darry could be a bit nicer. I think Ponyboy is the youngest and needs to have a friend, not an overbearing brother.

Julie: John, I have not heard from you yet. What do you think about what Dominique said?

Jackson: I know how Ponyboy feels. I have a mean brother, too, and he makes me mad.

Julie: I like the way you're thinking about the story. Does anyone else have something to add? (*There is no response, so Julie continues with another question.*)

When conducting these conversations, I felt the class was being productive and that I was able to get ideas of how well the students understood the text. However, when the principal dropped by my classroom for an informal observation, she opened my eyes about a few things. Although at first glance, my conversations with the students seemed productive and engaging, the principal pointed out that it was productive and engaging *only* for the students who were engaged. The principal helped me realize that the other students were not involved in the conversation. Some hands went up in response to my questions, but not all students had the chance to respond due to the time constraints. Not only were there only a few students involved in the conversation, most of the communication was teacher to student. The students rarely commented on each other's ideas. Some students hid from the conversation. It's relatively easy for students to hide when they are one of 27 people supposedly having a conversation.

"Why did they hide?" was the question I had to find answers to. Did they fail to do their reading? Did they not understand the novel because it was well above their reading capabilities? Were they bored with the story because they were not challenged enough by the text?

I needed to answer these questions to move my assessment and teaching forward. Obviously, I could not interact deeply with all 27 students in one whole-group discussion. The idea of moving to small groups was my first step in making changes to the way I taught. The intimate setting of small-group instruction that happens in guided reading helped me do just that. No one was able to hide in guided reading and I could assess each member's comprehension in the moment and make a decision to immediately support the student who needed support.

One of the main goals of the guided reading program is to pair students with books that are slightly difficult for them to read on their own. Students need to stretch, but not overextend, their literacy muscles. Form groups of students in approximately the same reading abilities so they can support each other's growth as readers.

Guided reading meetings provide an abundance of information that you can use to dynamically regroup students throughout the year, so try to avoid getting caught up in trying to create perfect groups at the start. Find a quick means of initially identifying students' skills so you can get them reading together as soon as possible.

The assessments outlined here can be used as both starting points and check-ups. Typically, you should reassess students who are below grade level more frequently to more closely monitor their progress. Remember, you will be continually assessing the students based on their responses in the group meetings and to their self-selected readings in one-to-one discussions. As you review their written responses to texts, you will glean more information about their abilities to comprehend and synthesize. As you listen to their conversations in group meetings, you will be able to evaluate their mastery of specific reading strategies. And as you listen to them articulate insights about books, you will be measuring their skills of expression. These authentic, embedded assessments will complement the more formal evaluations that you may decide to use or may be required to use as a matter of school or district policy (Fountas and Pinnell 2001).

Some school districts use electronic evaluation programs such as the Scholastic Reading Inventory (SRI) (Scholastic 2007), or the STAR computer adaptive reading test (STAR 2007a) to gauge reading levels. These tools may be efficient for assessing an overall reading ability, but are not necessarily effective for revealing the *specific* strengths and weaknesses of each student. If these tests are not available to you, use a low-tech, personal approach—ask students to read a short passage aloud while you listen to their fluency and determine their words per minute. This sampling of student reading performance takes just a few minutes, but the findings can have benefits in the long term. During these brief interactions, you can focus totally on the student in front of you. You will observe how the individual responds to both you and the text, start to build relationships, and identify the strengths and limitations of the student's performance. You will also get a feel for your students as a group—the skills specific classes have in common, how much differentiation will be needed for each group, and what reading traumas or successes students have had in the past that you will need to triage. You can use the data and insights to inform parent conferences and identify students who may need additional supports from you or, in extreme cases, further assessment for learning disabilities. Appendix A provides selections from leveled books along with a series of questions that assess students' abilities to use the reading strategies.

Assessing Each Student

When teaching reading, it seems obvious to assess each student. When using the guided reading model in the middle grades, you may have to find a way to fit individual assessments into tight and outdated traditions and schedules. Making adjustments and accommodations for individual assessments is well worth the trouble. Without a specific assessment of each student's reading skills, you can't possibly reach every learner. Even if you use multiple books simultaneously in your reading classes, you must know which skills and strategies to focus on with each group and each student. And, to form effective groups, you need data to make good placements (Akhavan 2004).

Your knowledge of students' reading skills can also enrich their lives outside of school. Sometimes parents are distressed because of their children's academic struggles. They suspect that poor reading skills are the cause, but they don't know how to help. Good assessments can tell us if students have general gaps in comprehension or fluency, or perhaps they have fallen behind in recognizing and using literary devices or understanding the varied structures and terminology of expository texts. While pinpointing problems and removing barriers to learning, you also want to eliminate excuses for poor performance. If some families have internalized the idea that their children are poor readers and, thus, are incapable of excelling in science or social studies or math, work to raise their expectations by providing a more complete picture of the students' strengths and weaknesses. Often, the diagnosis of poor reader follows a student through school and becomes a crutch instead of a temporary condition.

Conversely, some parent conferences reveal unreasonable expectations for students or the reluctance to accept severe learning disabilities. Data from good assessments, particularly when these data are drawn from multiple forms of evaluation, gives you information to share and analyze together.

Finally, specific and ongoing assessments can help measure the effectiveness of your teaching practices. The guided reading model integrates ongoing assessment with the group work, so you won't need to formally reassess all students, as you did at the beginning of the school year. However, for struggling readers, or those with specific deficiencies that you are trying to address, follow-up assessments throughout the year can provide important feedback to you. Setting aside a day each quarter for this purpose is a reasonable and worthwhile goal.

"Assessment is often seen as external to instruction, but it is an essential part of teaching. Both teachers and students benefit from multiple forms of evaluation. While high-stakes tests rarely provide feedback that has instructional value, other forms of assessment can foster literacy development in adolescents."

(NCTE 2006)

Establishing a Classroom of Readers

Spend the first week of the new school year building a classroom culture of respect and getting the students reading and writing in short sessions so you can get to know each other and shake off the summer's rust. In the second week, begin assessing their reading skills. In addition to discovering your students' interests and abilities, you will set the stage for the guided reading model.

Treat the initial assessment session as your first group meeting, and explain to students that you need silence in the classroom so you can hear them read aloud individually. Also, introduce the self-selected reading process so students will have something to focus on while you meet with their peers. Use a mini-lesson to kick off the first few classes, and assign short writing tasks to tie the mini-lessons to the self-selected readings. In a typical week, conduct two mini-lessons (about 20 minutes total), and each day, spend about five minutes introducing the day's activities, and allot about five minutes for wrapping up each class. This scheduling leaves roughly four hours during the week for individual assessments. (See Chapter 5 for examples of schedules for the teacher and students.)

While the class is engaged in reading and writing independently, call students one by one to a table in the back of the room. Listen to them read quietly for about three minutes and take notes on their progress. Most students will need only one assessment. Others might need a second or even a third evaluation to determine their skill levels. Depending on class size and how well the time is flowing, you can finish the process in a week. If you fall behind (or have radically unequal class sizes), shorten or eliminate a mini-lesson for one or two classes. Don't worry about extending the assessments into a second week, if necessary, because all of the students are reading during class and this is time well spent. Remember, after the summer break, students need to get back into practice reading on their own for set periods of time.

Types of Assessment

Teacher-led Reading Assessment

Some school districts use prepackaged three-minute reading assessments, a quick and satisfactory resource for a middle school guided reading program. The three-minute assessments actually take about five minutes to administer, but they can be valuable tools for constructing guided reading groups. An example of such assessments is *3-Minute Reading Assessments: Word Recognition, Fluency & Comprehension: Grades 5–8* (Raskinski and Padak 2005).

These short reading assessments are great for measuring fluency, an important criteria for assigning students to a guided reading group. However, these assessments do not offer good insights about students' comprehension or their ability to use specific reading strategies. To fill this gap, develop additional questions to measure a student's comprehension and ability to apply the reading strategies.

Grade-level Text Assessment

Another way to measure students' reading levels is to see how they fare with authentic text—passages comparable to those they will encounter in the curriculum. Select a series of passages that present increasing challenges to the student. In assessing a seventh grader, for example, begin with a typical seventh grade text that should take about two to three minutes to read. Listen to the student read and follow along with a copy on which you can make notes. You will start identifying reading strengths and areas of development for each student. Going through these individual assessments helps alleviate some of the facelessness that comes with having a 150-student load.

This process is not as neat and packaged as the computer testing models, nor does it give you a specific number like a Lexile score to statistically analyze student reading growth. However, it does provide baseline information that allows you to begin the process of creating the homogeneous groups that are the core of the guided reading program. By analyzing the results for an entire class, or groups of classes, you can begin to identify trends that indicate group strengths or deficiencies. These trends provide further evidence you can use to determine placement of students in guided reading groups. (See Appendix C for examples of reading passages and accompanying questions.)

Teaching is both an art and a science. The computer adaptive tests that give specific Lexiles, grade level equivalencies, and percentile rankings represent the science. The teacher listening to an individual student respond to an authentic piece of text is the art. Unlike the computer testing situation, teachers can assess for many qualitative reading dimensions, including student confidence, insight, and emotional response.

These aspects of reading are not answered in a computer adaptive text, but they are vitally important to painting a full picture of a student's reading ability. Informal assessments contribute to turning probing, individualized questions into a robust, colorful, and detailed picture of a student's reading abilities. This process generally takes about five to seven minutes per student. It is time well spent.

Computer-based Reading Assessment

If your school district uses a computer-based reading assessment, then it will only take one class period for you to get a basic measurement of your students' skills. Many computerized programs provide each student's score on the Lexile Framework for Reading, a nationally accepted scale of reading ability and text difficulty. The Scholastic Reading Inventory (SRI) (2007) is a widely-used computer adaptive test.

After students take the test, which is designed to measure recognition and comprehension of text, they will receive a Lexile score or range. You can use this as an initial point of reference to establish guided reading groups at the start of the school year. However, keep in mind that the Lexile score does not reflect students' interests, their prior knowledge about different topics they might encounter in reading, or their ability to navigate varied text structures and understand themes or implied meanings. The full range of a student's reading comprehension, vocabulary, and fluency cannot be measured by computerized tests. Only highly skilled teachers can assess these aspects as they come to know students as individual learners.

Ongoing In-group Assessment

As you listen to students discuss and read books in guided group meetings and ask them pointed questions, you will gain more information about their progress and setbacks as readers. This knowledge is crucial for appropriate placement in groups, as well as instructive for adapting our lessons and groups throughout the school year. Students who performed well on the initial assessment may not develop as expected. Conversely, students who initially indicated lower reading functioning may flourish in the group setting. Frequent formative assessment gives you the information you need to make good decisions about guided reading support (Harvey and Goudvis 2000).

Observe this guided reading meeting between Julie and her seventh grade students who were reading *Crossing Jordan* (Fogelin 2002).

Julie: Authors reveal characters by showing us what the character says to other characters. On page 17, Seth says, "Only ethnics pierce their ears." After reading this, how does that make you feel about Seth? What can we say about his personality?"

Luke: I think Cassie's dad (Seth) is pretty racist. He is making judgments about other cultures. I'm thinking he's going to be trouble for Cassie and prevent her from being friends with Jemmie.

Chen: Yeah, I don't like him already. He's full of anger and ignorance.

Marty: Why doesn't he like people who wear earrings?

Latanya: I think what Seth meant is that black people and people of different cultures wear earrings and whites don't. He doesn't like people who are different than him, and he must think people who wear earrings are different.

Luke: Yeah, I know a lot of people who wear earrings, including some guys and they are not ethnic at all. So Seth doesn't know what he's talking about.

Julie: Marty, what do you think the author is trying to tell us about this character Seth?

Marty: I don't know… maybe Seth doesn't like earrings?

Julie: (*directed to Marty*) Has anyone ever made a judgment about you without really knowing you?

Marty: I can't really think of anything right now.

Julie: Okay, do you think that Seth is being very unfair by saying that only certain types of people wear earrings?

Marty: Yeah, I guess.

Julie: Everyone turn to page 9. Here Seth says, "With them the men run off." To whom is he referring?"

Paula: He's talking about African American women. He's saying that all African American men leave their families and are irresponsible. It's not true. He is making an unfair judgment.

Julie: Do you think Seth is a bad person for saying this?

Chen: No, the things he says makes you mad but it makes you want to read further. I don't think Seth's a bad person because sometimes people can say racist things because they don't know any better. Once they learn what they said or what they did hurt someone, they change their behavior.

Julie: As you read further, stop and think about the instances of racist remarks or actions that occur in the story. What do these remarks tell you about the character who says them? How do you feel about the character after you read these remarks? Expand on your thoughts in your reader's journal so when we meet again, we can discuss this further.

From the conversation, Julie realized that Marty was having trouble making inferences about characters. She followed up with him during a quick meeting during silent reading time and used that moment to explicitly teach him about how readers get to know characters. For example, readers think about what the characters say and do and they infer characters' motivations. Julie also pointed out other instances in the book where Seth was overtly racist and helped Marty prepare his oral and written response for the next guided reading meeting. As the meetings progressed, Marty's comprehension was helped by the other members in his group.

Guided reading meetings provide the teacher with invaluable information about student reading needs that drives on-going assessment. For example, in Marty's case Julie knew that he was weak in his ability to make inferences. She had another guided reading group where the students were in need of instruction on making inferences. Consequently, Julie noted that Marty would be a better fit in this group where the next book would be studied. By this process, Julie is able to make adjustments that support the individual's learning needs. Assessment isn't only about initially placing students in groups; it's about the continual, dynamic analysis of student reading growth (Fountas and Pinnell 2001).

We use a variety of strategies to assess what our students are able and not able to do. In this regard, our approach reflects categories of formative assessment that Heritage describes as "on-the-fly, planned-for interaction, and curriculum-embedded assessment" (2007). Each means of collecting information gives greater insights into our students and what we need to do to provide effective instruction.

Reflections on Adolescent Literacy

Read the following quotation. Then answer the questions below.

"An assessment activity can help learning if it provides information that teachers and their students can use as feedback in assessing themselves and one another and in modifying the teaching and learning activities in which they are engaged" (Black et al. 2004).

1. Which types of assessment activities have you used that provide information to "help learning"? Of these, which have you found to be most practical in helping students understand what they need to do to improve their learning?

2. In what ways are your assessment activities comparable to those that Julie and Mark use in the guided reading model?

3. What ideas do you now have for strengthening your assessment activities?

Fundamentals of Guided Reading

Chapter 4

In the Classroom with *Julie*

I approached Chandra, an eighth grader, to discuss her new group book assignment. Chandra was sitting alone at her desk and she seemed upset. I was not sure why. When I created the new groups for this round of guided reading, I assigned Chandra to a group of students she had not worked with before. I had discussed the practice of changing groups with the whole class and small groups many times.

Julie: What do you think about your group book, Chandra?

Chandra: The book is fine.

Julie: What's bothering you, then?

Chandra: Well, I just don't feel good about being put in this book. It seems too easy.

I knew that Chandra had been assigned to a book with a slightly lower Lexile level. It was not a significantly lower Lexile book, but Chandra must have perceived that she was in a group with "struggling" readers. I had planned to discuss what I had hoped Chandra would do in the group when the group met again, but I realized that I needed to address it now.

Julie: Chandra, you are a terrific reader and that is one of the reasons you are in this group.

Chandra: Mrs. Donnelly, I know these kids in this group don't read as well as the other groups.

Julie: Exactly. Most of the kids in your new group are not as good at making inferences as you are. They need someone like you to point some things out to them. I could do it, but you know kids sometimes don't listen to the teacher.

Chandra: You know I don't like to talk about the books.

I laughed to myself. Chandra was forcing me to be very explicit about my thinking about her reading—something I should have done without Chandra prompting me.

Julie: I do know that, Chandra. That is why I put you in this group. You are strong in all aspects of your reading, except talking about your thinking. You will understand things some of the other kids won't, and you'll have to describe it to them. It will be good for you and good for them. Okay?

Chandra: (*smiling*) Mrs. D., sometimes I think you just try to come up with ways to torture me.

Julie: I wouldn't ask you to do it if I didn't know you could. It's time you take the lead.

Chandra: Okay, Mrs. D. I'll do it.

In another interaction later that year, Maya, a sixth grade student, approached me with a request.

Maya: Mrs. Donnelly, I want to be in *The Dark Hills Divide* (Carman 2005) book. That story seems so awesome.

I looked at Maya, quickly deciding how to handle this situation. Maya was a somewhat reluctant reader and she was often off task during silent reading. She did not always finish her assignments. *The Dark Hills Divide* would be a very challenging book for her.

Julie: Why do you want to read it, Maya? Your guided reading book, I think, is perfect for you.

Maya: Mrs. Donnelly, all my friends who have read *The Dark Hills Divide* say it is great. Plus, most of my friends in this class are assigned to that book.

I thought about my options and what would be best for Maya. Both Lexile scores and classroom observations indicated that Maya should be in the lower Lexile book. She had not shown a disposition to read. It would be a real challenge for her. But she seemed very motivated. Maya interrupted my thoughts.

Maya: Pleeasse, Mrs. Donnelly. Pleeasse.

I relented, but I was determined to leverage Maya's desire to read the book.

Julie: Okay, Maya, you can read the book. But here is what you need to promise me. You will have reading homework every night. You are going to have to work hard to keep up with this reading. You need to talk to me *before* our meetings if you have any questions. If you don't do this, I'm going to have to move you out of the group.

Maya: Thanks, Mrs. Donnelly, I will, I will, I will. I promise!

Julie: I'm counting on you, Maya.

I was pleasantly surprised with Maya's performance in the group. She not only read *The Dark Hills Divide* and kept up with her work, but she also finished the entire series. Maya did not become the perfect reading student, but she was very engaged in her reading for a period of time.

These two interactions show how the guided reading can be adapted to meet the needs of individual students. Although both students were assigned to books that did not specifically meet their assessed reading levels, I made a conscious decision to put them in situations that would support their specific needs.

Grouping Strategies

Students may be grouped in several ways in the guided reading model. The most practical and logical is the initial grouping based upon student reading abilities. However, there are times when you should take into account several other factors, such as student reading attitudes and developmental needs. For example, Julie's decision to let Maya join the group that was reading *The Dark Hills Divide* enforces the idea that students need to read personally interesting material (Oldfather 1993).

Through guided reading, you want to deepen literacy skills and place students according to their best advantage, but you also want to be developmentally appropriate and consider the broader goals of learning. In the middle grades, students have a wide range of academic, social, and emotional needs that teachers must address throughout the year. Dynamic reading groups give us the greatest flexibility, enabling us to change the composition and the focus of our lessons as students' skills develop. Ongoing assessment is a crucial part of the process involved in sustaining dynamic reading groups.

Guided reading differs from whole-group methods of teaching that are commonly found in middle school classrooms. Whole group teaching typically uses teacher-selected novels and a literature anthology, and provides limited, if any, opportunity for students to self-select reading materials (Worthy, Moorman, and Turner 1999). In middle school, many classes are taught using a "one-size-fits-all" textbook and instructional practices. In contrast, guided reading, by using a range of materials and grouping arrangements, aims to create readers who are engaged, strategic, versatile, and confident about their choices and interpretations of what they read.

Initial Grouping

As discussed in Chapter 3, you will form the initial groups based on the beginning-of-the-year assessment. Decisions about how to group students and what to focus on in each meeting require a fairly in-depth knowledge of your students. The guided reading model provides many opportunities to build that awareness. Within the first few weeks of school, you will have completed the initial assessments, which may include one-on-one or computerized assessment tools. By the end of the first session of guided reading meetings, you will have interacted with each student about half a dozen times. By the end of the school year, you will have had many structured opportunities to meet with students individually or in small groups. You watch them interact with their peers and the text. You see them as they think through a problem. You occasionally share a laugh at a character in the book—or sometimes

"Middle school reading instruction is full of mixed messages and inconsistency. Importantly, students are expected to become independent readers, yet they get limited opportunities to explore their own interests in reading, to read at their own pace, or to make their own decisions about whether or not to read a book."

(Ivey and Broaddus 2001)

a character in the reading group. In addition, as you circulate through the classroom during silent reading time, you can have informal one-on-one conversations. The data that you collect in these situations gives you the power to modify lessons to meet students' needs. As a result, you are able to steer a group in another direction, based not on a pre-set worksheet or your own desires, but on what you have discovered about your students. This guided reading model places the individual student at the center of reading—an emphasis on students as individuals that is one hallmark of effective middle school instruction.

How many groups?

In an ideal world, you would have about five groups of no more than five students reading a book that was focused specifically on what each group needs. However, with most class sizes exceeding 30 students, it may be better to establish more guided reading groups rather than place a larger number of students in the groups. Ideally, groups should have no more than six students. Why is six the magic number? This limit is solely based upon our own experiences as teachers who have taught guided reading for the past several years. With more than six members, it becomes difficult to successfully facilitate the guided reading conversation and allow every member to speak. The conversations become forced and the guided reading experience tends to morph into a question-answer situation rather than a natural-sounding conversation.

How many books?

One solution to making the guided reading manageable is to have two groups of students reading the same novel while differentiating the instruction for that one novel. Level the novels and describe them as being appropriate for developing readers, grade level readers, and advanced readers. For example, there may be times when 12 students in a class may all read at the same level but have different social and emotional needs. This situation offers a great opportunity to have the students read the same novel but participate in two separate guided reading groups. Although the ability groups are similar, the students in each will actually require a different focus of instruction.

Same book, different focus

Some groups may be reading the same title but have a very different reading experience. For example, the novel *Crossing Jordan* by Adrian Fogelin provides differentiated reading experiences for students. On the surface, this is a relatively simple and familiar story of two adolescent girls of different races who become friends. They must deal with family members trying to keep them apart while they forge their friendship. On one hand, the story can be taught for basic comprehension and story elements. For a group that still needs to shore up comprehension, the lessons can be focused on those aspects. However, the book also lends itself to an analysis of symbolism. For students who are ready for understanding literary devices and deeper comprehension, we insert these concepts into brief lessons at the start of the group meeting and make them a focus of student note-taking during reading.

Dynamic Grouping

Initially, base your grouping decisions on information you have gathered about reading fluency and responses to comprehension questions. Subsequent decisions for dynamic grouping are built on data, but also incorporate more of the art of teaching. Making appropriate decisions requires knowledge of the mysterious world of young adolescents—where sixth grade boys want to avoid girls but by the eighth grade, they actively compete for the girls' attention; and where students of all stature rise to heights of joy and fall to dungeons of despair based on approval or perceived slights. As in Julie's example regarding Maya's request to join the *The Dark Hills Divide* reading group, there are times when you may group friends together to stimulate the conversation and times when you may separate friends to avoid complacency or cliques. You need to encourage quiet students to talk, stretch students who are static, and maximize the productivity of your teaching given a limited number of book titles to choose from. You will find that you are constantly tweaking your groups. Dynamic guided reading groups help teachers develop the field vision of a baseball manager: deftly moving players a few yards here or there, sending a runner to third, or taking a role-player and giving him or her a more prominent position. The only thing you *can't* do is cut a player from your team. There are additional sources of information you can use to ensure that the guided reading groups are dynamic, as noted here.

Student interest in a topic or book

Interest can be a key factor in a student's choice of reading material and willingness to read a text that the teacher may think is too difficult. One of Mark's students asked to be placed in the *White Fang* (London 1991) reading group because her sister had raved about how great the book was. Mark, concerned that the book was beyond the student's reading level, attempted to redirect her by recommending other interesting books. She was undeterred. Mark pointed out that the book she wanted to read might be challenging and long. She said she would get a copy and read at home. Mark finally relented and placed her in the *White Fang* group, hopeful that the student's strong desire would be a match for the difficult text.

Of course, he paid extra attention to the student during the guided reading sessions. He checked in with her often to see how her reading was coming and provided extra direction for the first few meetings. It quickly became clear that such precautions were unnecessary. The student became one of the leaders of the reading group. Her enthusiasm for the book was contagious, and she was active in the discussions. As a result, she gained a great deal of confidence in talking about books, where previously, she had been quiet and reserved. This willingness to fully participate fostered her ability to think about the text critically. Obviously, Mark's decision to let her join the *White Fang* group was beneficial for this student.

"Choice should be meaningful. Reading materials should be appropriate and should speak to adolescents' diverse interests and varying abilities."

(NCTE 2007)

Although other students make similar requests to try books that are out of their obvious range, you do not always need to acquiesce. Take into account the reasons why they want to stretch and your growing knowledge of their developmental needs. If the response is simply, "The book looks cool," try giving them a copy to read for a day and see if they remain interested. More often than not, they return the original book and are satisfied with your grouping decision.

Creating leaders

Language arts class is not just about reading and writing. It also teaches students how to express thoughts clearly using the spoken word. Some students who do quite well when they are speaking directly to the teacher lack the confidence to express themselves in small groups. One tactic that the guided reading model allows is placing a student in a group where the level of the focused book is slightly lower than the student's reading comprehension level. Although this sounds counter to the goal of placing students in the right reading range, a temporary assignment with easier material can bolster a student's confidence and foster development of other language arts skills.

Tell students that you know the book itself will not be a real challenge, but that you want them to serve as a model for other students. The designated students' jobs in this group is to speak out and jump in when the group struggles, and that they will be kicking off the conversation. This set-up serves two purposes. First, by giving the selected students texts they can capably read, you reduce their fear of saying something wrong about the books. Second, when you let students know that their placement in a group is due to their (relatively) strong reading skills, you boost their confidence. Typically, when these students later encounter more challenging books, they respond by increasing their participation in the group's discussions.

Introducing a stronger reader into a group can also boost the confidence of the existing members. The students take you at our word when, at the beginning of the year, you explain that groups will change. Some students are strong at certain things and some at other things. At times, a short book may be much more challenging than a longer book. A book that is easy to read may actually be harder to understand because students are looking at why an author does certain things. Some students may read quickly but not understand as well as others, and vice versa. The groups will change.

Inside the Guided Reading Meetings

Teachers who are new to guided reading usually have many questions about how the meetings work. In this section we consider questions that we have been asked most frequently and which reflect teachers' concerns as they embark on implementing new instructional procedures. These questions will serve as a launching pad for a detailed examination of the heart of guided reading—the group meetings.

How long should a guided reading group discussion last?

The short answer is about 15 minutes. Although it may be tempting to let the discussion continue beyond this time frame, stay focused on the specific goals for each meeting. The reading group discussion is not a literature circle; consequently, the students do not drive the entire conversation. On occasion, students may spontaneously say something profound and you will decide to "go with it," setting aside your plan to nudge the group's comprehension to a deeper level. Here's an example of how Julie handled one such moment during a guided reading of *A Wrinkle in Time* by Madeleine L'Engle (1962). Julie allowed this particular conversation to continue past the allotted 15 minutes. It was a golden teaching moment, and the students were probing the theme of this book.

"Caring, responsive classroom environments enable students to take ownership of literacy activities and can counteract negative emotions that lead to lack of motivation."

(NCTE 2007)

Lesson Focus: Authors manipulate the setting in a scene to create a certain mood or feeling for their readers.

Julie: You all have read up to Chapter 7 in *A Wrinkle in Time.* Let me begin the conversation by asking: What struck you as you read this chapter?

Avi: I thought it was weird when Meg, Charles Wallace, and Calvin landed on Camazotz and everything looked hazy. It gave me a creepy feeling.

Julie: What about this setting made you feel creepy?

Avi: Everything is the same. The little children are bouncing balls in sync. One boy drops his ball and the mom sort of freaks out and rushes out to get him and pull him inside the house. It was so evil.

Claire: What's so evil about being the same?

At this point Julie decided to set aside her initial lesson about the setting and purposely facilitate this discussion about evil to deepen the students' understanding of the book.

Julie: Great question, Claire. What is so evil about being the same? There wouldn't be any conflict or anyone picking on you because of your clothes, hair, etc.

Franklin: Yeah, but it still is evil.

Julie: Why?

Franklin: If you don't have any individuality, then life would be boring and anyone could control you because you don't think about things.

Claire: But you wouldn't care because you would be just like everyone else and happy, right?

Franklin: How can you know if you're happy if you don't know what pain and sadness are?

Planning is required to ensure that guided reading sessions run smoothly. Follow these four steps in your planning for effective planning.

Step One: Know what the book offers

Of course, you will need to read the books that they teach in the guided reading groups. Reading the book to analyze the teaching points that present themselves is the first step in having an effective conversation with your students. However, there are many other factors that must be simultaneously considered when planning for a guided reading lesson. These include having a firm knowledge of the language arts standards, a solid understanding of reading strategies and genre elements, and a clearly defined lesson outcome. In addition to these factors, you must rely on your observations of student literacy behaviors and use those observations to decide how to differentiate instruction based on students' social and developmental needs.

Step Two: Have a plan

Any group discussion can be tricky to manage if you are not prepared for each lesson. Spend about 15 minutes meeting with each guided reading group. It isn't much time, so it is imperative that you revisit the text before you teach it. Because group discussions are dynamic, you need to be prepared to latch on to spontaneous teaching moments that may arise in any given meeting.

Step Three: Manage the conversations

As the leader of the group, you can direct or redirect the conversation as needed. Middle school students are notorious for wanting to stall a conversation because they really like the individual attention they get from small group discussions. Although this seems like a truly wonderful experience that you may not want to stop, you do have a lesson goal to reach and a time schedule to maintain. Here are a couple of ways to honor students' comments while keeping the discussion on track:

- Try ending the conversation by saying, "I'm very pleased with your enthusiasm. Take some time to think about what you learned from this meeting as you record your thinking in your reader's journal in preparation for the next meeting. When would you like to meet again?"

- To build on a keen insight while being mindful of time, schedule consecutive meetings with enthusiastic groups for the very next class period in order to continue the conversation. Mark allows certain groups to take their meeting to the next level and reconvene in the library for further discussion without him.

Read below to see how this played out in one of Mark's classes.

Mark: All of you have done a great job responding to your books and doing your assignments so far. I'm very impressed with your ability to stay focused, so I want to give you the opportunity to have your own book club meeting in the library. You all just read Part Two in *The Stone Goddess* (Ho 2005) and you are ready to have a discussion. Here's your pass; you can go to the library.

Chelsea: (*visibly excited and giving a high five to her friend, Chen*) Oh cool, we'll be sure to talk about the book all the time, Mr. Donnelly.

Chen: Are you for real? You trust us to meet on our own?

Mark: Yes, I trust you, but since I won't be there, I would like you to write two paragraphs about what you learned from your meeting in your reader's notebook.

Nate: Oh, snap! This is so awesome!

Mark: I would like you to return in about 20 minutes.

Mark took a chance, and for this group of students his message was extremely motivating. He had spoken to the librarian beforehand about keeping an eye on the book club. As the class progressed, Mark lost track of the 20-minute time frame. He was ready to send another student after the book club members when they arrived back just as the bell rang. He never had a chance to check in with them.

During lunch, Mark went to the library to get a report from his colleague. The librarian said the students chatted about the book for the whole hour. When he walked by to check in with them, they were comparing the two legends in the book. The next day, Mark spoke to his students and asked about the discussion. Sure enough, they confirmed the librarian's report.

Chelsea: We compared the two legends that are in the story.

Mark: For the entire hour?

Chen: Yeah, Nate said the new legend made a better story but I disagreed with him because it's boring and it didn't move the story along.

Sara: The first legend was confusing and I didn't understand what the ogre stood for. But then Chen said the ogre stood for the Communist Party who just wanted everyone to bring stuff to them and aren't willing to work for it themselves, but Nate didn't agree.

The conversation continued, and Mark knew they had indeed engaged in a thoughtful discussion. His quick assessment was reinforced by the reading responses he later reviewed in their notebooks. You may find that sixth graders generally do better than eighth graders when they are permitted to leave the classroom for book discussions. Older students may be more likely to stray off task, so you may want to be more careful about their meetings outside the classroom.

Keep in mind that you need to meet with other groups and you have only 45–55 minutes to accomplish this and many other tasks. If you let one group monopolize your time, you are doing a disservice to the other groups. They will be disappointed and you will get far behind in your own work as a result.

Step Four: Stay on track

Guided reading is not just a few students and a teacher sitting around talking about a story. To an untrained eye it may seem that way, but the process goes deeper. Facilitating a guided reading meeting requires constant engagement from the teacher and a series of purposeful and thoughtful decisions about how to leverage students' comments while keeping an eye on the larger goals for each session. Specifically, the teacher is trying to increase students' comprehension of text that is slightly difficult for them to read alone. This task requires a highly-skilled teacher who is constantly focused on what is happening in the group (Fountas and Pinnell 2001).

During a guided reading meeting, the teacher assesses student understanding, facilitates a meaningful conversation by making sure all members of the group have a voice, repairs comprehension breakdowns, and takes advantage of teachable moments based on student responses. The teacher also continually redirects students back to the text and builds on their existing comprehension strategies to lead them to a higher level of understanding (Fountas and Pinnell 2001). If the conversation goes on too long, students begin to lose focus. Keep in mind that students are reading chunks of the novels or nonfiction texts, so 10–15 minutes for a session will be adequate in most cases. After 10–15 minutes middle school students will begin to repeat themselves and struggle to actively listen.

On the opposite end of the spectrum of guided reading discussions, teachers must resist the urge to transmit knowledge to the students by continually asking direct questions. The emphasis should be on guiding, encouraging students to think deeply so that, as much as possible, they can form their own conclusions about the meaning of the text. Otherwise, the guided reading group will morph into the more limited, traditional format where the teacher in a small-group setting quizzes students on the text and no authentic conversation takes place.

Logistical Considerations

Managing the logistics of groups in a classroom can be a challenging task, particularly when you are working with a small group of students and others are engaged independently in other activities. Other logistical considerations include grading student performance and managing homework assignments.

How many groups can a teacher meet with in one class period?

It is possible to meet with two to three guided reading groups per 45–55 minute class period. This process runs smoothly with good classroom management techniques such as those described in Chapter 5, and thoughtful lesson planning. Students who are not currently meeting in a group can be reading silently and writing in response to their reading.

How can the members of a guided reading group talk without disturbing the whole class?

When students enter or leave a guided reading meeting it is important that they are very quiet so as not to disturb the other readers in the classroom. Transitions are something to practice during the first part of the school year. Within a short time, students should be able to return to their seat without much noise.

Guided reading meetings usually occur in a corner of the classroom. Because of the size of middle school students, finding adequate space for them to be both in the classroom but distant from other students can be challenging. Arranging a few folding chairs in the back of the room usually suffices. Ideally, you will be gathered closely together so you won't have to speak loudly to hear each other. In guided reading meetings, show students how to speak to each other using "12-inch voices", meaning only speaking loud enough to be heard a foot away.

These effective group dynamics do not happen without explicit work. You must spend time developing the guided reading culture, particularly if you are teaching in a school district that does not use the guided reading model from elementary grades through middle school.

How many days a week does a teacher meet with guided reading groups?

It is reasonable for a teacher to meet with all the guided reading groups at least once a week, and often twice. Of course, this will depend on the number of groups in a class. You can devote three days to scheduled guided reading meetings and use the remaining days for activities with the whole group: for example, vocabulary study, silent reading, or writing.

Can students be graded in guided reading?

Grading can be very straightforward. Students need to have read the assigned text and have a pencil or pen to take notes. Their reader's notebooks and any other written assignment must be completed. Ask students to open their journals and do a quick check-in during the first minute of the meeting. Collect their journals periodically for a more in-depth review at a later date. The initial check-in is just to make sure the student is prepared. You may want to record the grade as part of class participation points. Grading in middle school is a constant balancing act between fostering the students' love of reading and writing and teaching them to be responsible for their work. Our goal is to help students learn to become better readers and writers by showing them what to do next to improve their comprehension, not to just arbitrarily assign grades to their work (Romano 1987).

Keep a Guided Reading Record Sheet for every group you meet with, and record student comments so that you can address any comprehension breakdown immediately during the meeting. The sheet includes the members' names, an area for the teacher's comments and student quotes, as well as a space for points that are awarded for being prepared. Offer three to five points for each guided reading meeting. (Find a template for this record sheet in Appendix A.)

When middle school students know they will be meeting in a small group and reading text that is at their instructional level, they usually take full advantage of the time you give them in class to read. Their urgency to be ready for each meeting really complements the overall classroom management methods of guided reading. It provides incentive to the students to stay focused and use their time well.

Ideally, students will have substantial time to read *each* day in class. For some students, your classroom provides the only opportunity they will have to read in a quiet environment. If your school does not have dedicated time for silent reading, try to offer these opportunities to students. Keeping the book in the classroom guarantees that it will not be lost or forgotten.

What do you do if a student does not complete an assignment?

The guided reading assignment also serves as a beginning talking point for shy or reluctant students. Because you only have 10–15 minutes together, students need to come to the group ready to share their thoughts. There is little time for them to *not* know what to say. If you are met with a blank stare, you have the option to refer the students back to what they have previously written and prepared. It soon becomes apparent if the student has not completed the assignment. This information informs your next move. Your response depends on the reason why a student may come to the guided reading group without a completed assignment. Assuming that the student has not been absent, immediately address the matter in a congenial but serious manner. You do not want students to "shut down and mope" during the meeting, but you do want them to realize that this cannot happen again because of the responsibilities each individual has within the group. Ask the student to listen attentively to what the other group members have to say. Sometimes, you may require the student to meet with another group member later to catch up on the assignment. The student will be explicitly told that no points will be awarded for that guided reading meeting. After one or two times, students rarely come to the meetings unprepared. Whatever the excuse for not completing the assignment, this approach allows you to address why the work was not complete before a long passage of time has occurred. It's much more difficult for students to "hide" or "fake" reading when they are among six members of a guided reading discussion than when they are in a whole-class discussion.

Where does homework fit in?

Establishing a homework connection is easy in guided reading meetings. To maintain cohesiveness, teach guided reading as a genre study. Create a system that requires students to read two books within the same genre during a guided reading unit. One book is their self-selected book from the school library, and the other is the guided reading book, which you have selected.

One reason to have students read two texts is to manage a quiet classroom during silent reading. Students read at different paces, but no matter how quickly students read, they will always have a book to focus on in the classroom. For example, students who finish the guided reading book assignment early can move to their self-selected books. In the event that students claim to have forgotten the self-selected text at home, direct them to choose a comparable book from your classroom library that is organized according to genres. With a library book or self-selected text, students can have a book to read for homework and you do not have to worry about losing a guided reading book. Ask students to read for about 30 minutes a night and write two to three paragraphs of their thinking in their reader's notebooks.

Another reason for students to read two books within the same genre is to create opportunities for them to construct meaning from what they read by noticing the common elements of each book. Have students compare the two texts in the form of a reading letter or essay test at the end of the reader's workshop genre study unit. This reading letter builds upon the concepts that were taught about the genre and allows students to expand their knowledge of both their specific text and the genre in general. The test, typically taken in one class

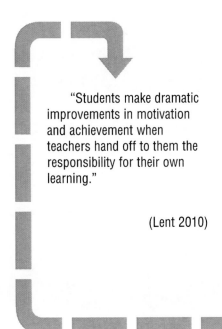

"Students make dramatic improvements in motivation and achievement when teachers hand off to them the responsibility for their own learning."

(Lent 2010)

period, can serve as good practice in test taking, integrates purposeful writing into the reading unit, and provides an additional assessment opportunity. Typically, the topics for these writing letters can focus on a number of literary elements. Since students are already reading two books at one time, keep the letters simple and only assign one topic per reading letter. This allows students to go in depth about a particular topic rather than glossing over every element. Provide a range of topics so that by the end of the school year, students will have had opportunities to explore various features of literary genres. These topics are based on Lattimer (2003) and outlined in the chart on the following page.

You want students to become engaged, independent readers who will know how to make sense of what they read as a result of their experiences with classmates in guided reading groups. Your aim is to provide a learning environment that fosters student participation and motivation, one that takes into consideration the developmental and personal differences among your students.

Features of Literacy Genres

Topics for the Reading Letter Essay

Character Analysis

- Are the characters believable?
- What is the character's point-of-view?
- Describe how the character acts around other characters.
- Describe both the positive and negative personality traits of the character.

Conflict

- What is the main conflict of the story?
- What are the characteristics of the conflicts used in this genre?
- How does the author introduce the conflict?
- How is the conflict resolved?

Plot

- How is the plot sequenced?
- How does the author show movement of time?
- Which time movement techniques were most effective? Why?

Style

- How did the author reveal the characters to the reader?
- What was the tone of the story?
- How does the author show perspective?

Reflections on Adolescent Literacy

"Students in the middle grades and beyond are not only developing as readers and writers, but also beginning to explore possible identities and a range of personal interests about the world" (Ivey and Broaddus 2001).

1. What do the behaviors of students in your classes reveal about their individual identities as well as their development as readers and writers? To what extent does desire for conformity with the group affect the behaviors and attitudes of your students and their response to literacy activities?

2. What do you think are the advantages of the guided reading model for accommodating the needs of adolescent readers?

3. Logistical factors play an important role in the extent to which a classroom functions effectively and efficiently. What logistical factors, if any, have been problematic for you and how have you addressed the situations?

Organizing for Guided Reading

Chapter 5

In the Classroom with **Mark**

Outside the classroom window, the ground is covered in white. Trees in the distance droop from the weight of an early snowfall. Inside the classroom a student is nestled under a table below the window with his hoodie pulled over his head. Another student sits with feet comfortably on a desk. Another has found a great spot in the corner, with her back supported by both walls. Three other students share a small rug behind a reading table. At the table, I am meeting with six students who are immersed in quiet conversation about the novel. When I am through guiding them to a deeper understanding of the book, I release them to work individually at their desks, and another group of students quietly assembles at the table to meet with me. This routine continues until the bell rings. Students then place their novels on the assigned shelf, tuck their guided reading notebooks in their binders, and exit the room. The room remains calm and quiet throughout the process.

Achieving a classroom culture of readers doesn't happen overnight. It involves *explicit* teaching of the desired behaviors, consistency in reinforcing those behaviors, and a lot of practice. In September, a visitor would see something very different. The classroom would definitely not be so quiet and calm.

There are almost as many ways to manage a classroom as there are teachers, and we don't presume to have a strategy for every situation. But experience has shown us that adopting effective classroom management techniques is crucial to the success of the guided reading model. Just as important, guided reading encourages good classroom management.

While the guided reading classroom is free-flowing and student directed, it is also structured. Every decision is deliberate, filtered through the lens of our primary objectives of maximizing student reading time, minimizing distractions, and facilitating thoughtful interactions among students in the groups.

Silent Means Silent

The silent treatment might seem severe, but it is a necessary part of an authentic reading experience. To encourage students to get lost in a book means providing the right environment for sustained reading (Atwell 2007). If they are allowed to speak to others, if others speak to them, or if other people are speaking around them, they cannot be fully engaged in reading.

During the group meeting, other students are reading silently. Because at least one group will always be talking, limit other noises. Extraneous conversations can create a critical mass of distraction that undermines the guided reading model. Another reason for maintaining silence is that it serves to nudge reluctant readers in the right direction. Sometimes, no matter what you do, students who are intent on *not* reading will fulfill their ambition. They will stare at the book, out the window, or at the wall. However, by removing all other options (of course, drawing and sleeping are not allowed) for the vast majority of reluctant readers, any book becomes more interesting than the tile on the ceiling. When you can't talk, you can't bother the person next to you. And if you can't draw, you might as well read. Silence means silence; anything else and the program will not be effective. Sustaining silence requires vigilance and consistency, but once the right culture is established, students will read.

At the beginning of every school year, practice whispering. It is a simple but essential lesson. Stand on one side of the classroom and select a student to stand as far away from you as possible. Then ask the student to speak in a whisper loud enough to hear from a distance. Of course, the student usually starts out whispering at the decibel level of a yell, but give the student time to get quieter and quieter until the student's voice registers the right softness. As the student modeling the task practices lowering his lung power, his peers will grow quiet because they are trying to hear what is being said. Finally, the entire class becomes silent except for you and the student having the "whisper conversation." Then identify a few reasons why students should keep this whispering method in mind.

Even a whisper can be too loud when people are concentrating on reading. Although whispering is quiet, it is not silent. Students really understand this point during their first guided reading conversation when they see that whispering in the classroom does indeed disturb others. If they do not reach this conclusion independently, they will usually acknowledge that 10 people whispering would be disruptive to the class. Therefore, it is unfair to start a conversation at any time when others are engaged in reading.

If students are not on task during reading workshop, it can be helpful to issue a series of warnings that result in progressive discipline. Offer progressive reinforcements; for example, a class that has done well will have five minutes of free time at the end of the period. Consistency in applying the silent rule is essential. Early in the year, approach a student who is breaking this rule and quietly and respectfully explain that the next instance will result in a warning. It should not be necessary to report students for corrective action to the administration for inappropriate behavior during reading time. Perhaps they will need to serve a lunch detention if they have refused to do their work during the class period or send home a written note to their parents or guardians. For the most part, the students respond appropriately if they are treated respectfully.

Spread the Word About Silence

One of the more challenging aspects of running a middle school guided reading program is the presence of other adults. Many middle grade classrooms today have one or more co-teachers or assistants who are responsible for special education students. Sometimes parents or community volunteers may be present. It's crucial that all these adults understand your expectations, particularly regarding voice level. The students will buy into the need to have a quiet classroom. However, if other adults do not respect this aspect of the classroom culture, students' acceptance that the rules of silence are for their benefit will cease, and you will lose credibility.

Guided Reading and Teacher Collaboration

Mark has used the guided reading model successfully with different co-teachers and with students whose disabilities included Asperger's syndrome, autism, ADHD, oppositional defiant disorder, and behavior disorders. Typically, he might have eight to 12 special needs students in a class of 30. Together, he and the co-teacher assess the students' reading levels and developmental needs and place them in appropriate guided reading groups. Many of the students with learning disabilities function quite well in groups with advanced readers. The most positive aspect is that special education students are fully integrated into the reading groups. This enables both teachers to conduct reading groups simultaneously at times. Other times, one teacher monitors and supports the class as a whole while the other teacher guides a reading group. Co-teaching, often a source of frustration for both teachers, results in some of the most effective and satisfying instruction in Mark's career.

"But I Have a Good Excuse!"

Often, particularly in the first few weeks of school, students will not quite grasp the "totally silent" concept. To keep things fair and consistent, deal with *all* inappropriate student communication promptly. Some students will take offense at being reprimanded. They will say that they were pointing out something interesting in their book to a peer. Tell them they will have time to share at the end of class and to *hold onto that thought for later*. They will tell you they were answering a question from a student. Tell them they should ignore the other student. The same goes for requests for pencils, paper, books, or erasers.

Silent Communicating: Using Appropriate Hand Signals

In the last few years, it has become a part of popular culture to say, "talk to the hand," while holding up a palm to the other person. Although this can be seen as a rude gesture in public, it can actually be a fairly lighthearted way to deal with the problem of a student who is interrupting others. By flashing the hand to the errant student, a peer can send a message *without saying a word*. After teaching this trick to students, they can take responsibility for their own study habits without disrupting the rest of the class.

"Bleeding or on Fire"

So how do you get a middle school student to understand that what they have to say must be *extremely* important to interrupt the guided reading time? Tell them: "If it's really important, you may approach me and ask your question." Your interpretation of what is important may not match your students' interpretations, and you may be bombarded with requests for pencils, paper, and drinks of water. A master teacher gave us some advice: Tell the students not to interrupt the group meeting unless they're "bleeding or on fire." We used this example and later added "vomiting" to the list after several unfortunate interruptions.

What Are the Students Doing with Their Time?

Aside from the requirement of silence, the students have fairly wide latitude to determine how to use their time. When their group is meeting, they must attend and participate in the discussion. Because each meeting usually lasts no longer than 15 minutes, there will always be time during class for independent reading. We usually schedule one guided reading meeting a week per group. Each session includes a separate reading assignment that the students are expected to do in class. Because a guided reading group may have members with different fluency levels, one student might finish the group assignment while another needs more time. The student who reads more quickly will then have the choice of making notations and responses or reading a self-selected book. The same student also could note a "wonderful word" or work on an assignment (usually a writing response) from the self-selected book. There is always something constructive to do. After assignments are completed, pleasure reading kicks in.

Student Independence

The guided reading model provides many opportunities for students to practice self-reliance. They must take responsibility for completing assignments on their own. They must learn how to use their time wisely while juggling multiple assignments and reading multiple books simultaneously. And by not being able to communicate with each other outside of the guided reading group meetings, they must learn to look inward for motivation and guidance.

The need for independent work and self-direction becomes even more important because the teacher is not always available to help, seeing as the teacher is listening, monitoring, and overseeing the reading groups. Students need to know that they should not interrupt us during the group meetings. Encourage students to become more independent, but recognize that they still need individual attention. Setting aside time to circulate through the classroom while they are working and reading is one way to provide regular access. Designate a specific time for questions by letting students know when they can meet with you; for example, "I'll be available at the end of the hour," or "If it is quick, talk to me during the group change time." It is necessary to consistently provide options for access.

Requiring students to manage an increasingly complex workload is exactly what the majority of middle school students need. Typically, many students leave elementary school with a high degree of dependence on the teacher. As they move through the middle grades, in preparation for high school, they must learn to become more self-reliant and adaptable. The guided reading model provides a developmentally appropriate continuum of growth and responsibility, but it does not occur without work from the teacher. Specific supports include assigning and reviewing the reader's notebook entries, clearly communicating daily reading requirements, continually reviewing the guided reading meeting schedule, and creating a community of learners who are willing and know how to step in to help when someone has missed an assignment. This conscious cultivation of the classroom culture takes time, but is well worth the effort. The next sections describe tactics and resources to build an environment in which students understand and adhere to the rules.

The Reader's Notebook

The reader's notebook plays an important role in helping students to deepen their comprehension. Provide prompt questions to guide students as they think about what they have read; the responses they record become part of the discussion in the guided reading meeting. Having students routinely maintain their notebooks requires decisions about the format and logistics of managing the accumulation of papers that develops over time. It may take a fair amount of experimentation before finding a practical solution.

Spiral notebooks can be provided for all students to use during group meetings (intending that these be kept the whole year). The students take notes and are responsible for organizing their work. The notebooks

"We can all agree that meaningful schoolwork promotes students' learning of academic content. But why stop there? I believe that meaningful work can also teach students to love challenges, to enjoy effort, to be resilient, and to value their own improvement. In other words, we can design and present learning tasks in a way that helps students develop a *growth mindset*, which leads to not just short-term achievement but also long-term success."

(Dweck 2010)

can work well for guided reading. However, they can be expensive to purchase and replace when lost. Students also have a tendency to use the notebooks as an emergency source of paper—a repository for math equations, science diagrams, social studies maps and, of course, typical middle school notes dealing with typical middle school lives. At the other extreme, if students are required to manage their notes individually, most will keep the notes for a meeting or two, then the papers will slowly absorb into folders, binders, books, and piles found at the bottom of their lockers.

There is a tool which meets the requirements of being inexpensive, large enough to hold only one unit, easily replaced, and simple to construct from available supplies. Before starting a new book, have students take a few minutes to assemble a 10-page notebook. Counting out five lined, loose-leaf sheets of paper coupled with a few reproducible "thinking" sheets that focus on specific literary devices or reading comprehension skills works very well. Examples of the thinking sheets are provided in Appendix B. Covering the sheets with a large piece of construction paper finishes the job. The construction paper easily folds over the papers, creating a useful notebook for multiple guided reading meetings. Because it has little value beyond the classroom, the reader's notebook will not be recruited for other purposes.

In this folder, students first write their reading assignment, the focused questions from the teacher, and their responses to the selection. Then they can add details they personally discovered about the book, as well as observations shared by classmates in the group discussion. The folder also provides a source for teacher assessment, as well as a reference tool for students to use when they are writing their final essay about their guided reading book.

Peers Help Peers

With as many as six groups reading four different books and moving at different paces in four or five different classes, it becomes virtually impossible for a teacher to respond to the question, "What did we do yesterday? I was absent." With a typical five percent absentee rate, you would be going through this process seven or eight times a day. We do not suggest you attempt this.

Instead, expect students to find a reliable partner in their group. Talk with the students about how to choose a partner and provide assistance and support as needed, or assign one member, on a rotating basis, to be the record-keeper who copies the notes from the day's discussion onto a master agenda, to be used by anyone who is absent or who missed a meeting. The student who receives the help will, of course, be expected to return the favor. This method builds student independence and ownership of the learning process, while reinforcing the classroom culture of mutual assistance.

Even with help from their classmates, some students will need additional support. We are not advocating that you ignore them, only that you hold them responsible for first seeking help from a reliable peer. If a student still has questions about an assignment, then you need to be available to provide assistance.

"Observe any K–12 cafeteria and watch students huddle together over iPhones, handheld video game consoles, and MP3 players. Watch as they teach one another to sync, tweet, and tag. Although you might not recognize those terms, your students probably do. Ask them how they learned such skills, and they'll often say, 'It's obvious. Everybody knows that.'

What that really means is that the kids teach one another—so efficiently, so effortlessly, and so expertly that it doesn't even feel like learning."

(Jackson, Johnson, and Askia 2010)

Classroom Communication Tools

To help students stay aware of the overall structure and activities for guided reading groups, keep a chart prominently displayed at the front of the classroom. The required reading for each group book is listed on this chart. If a particular group is moving at a different pace, we adjust the notations accordingly. The chart enables students to see when their group will meet, exactly how far they should have read in a book, and when silent reading is scheduled. Figure 5.1 is an example of a management chart showing three groups reading different novels in the same genre.

Fig. 5.1. Guided Reading Management Chart

Title	Mon.	Tue.	Wed.	Thurs.	Fri.
A Wrinkle in Time	MEET	Pages 1–20	Pages 20–40	MEET	Silent reading
The Dark Hills Divide	Self-selected reading	MEET	Pages 1–24	Pages 24–50	Silent reading
Artemis Fowl	MEET	Pages 1–15	MEET	Pages 15–30	Silent reading
	Students are writing in response to their reading every day.				

Ask students to write all reading assignments in their reader's notebook. The reader's notebook, the posted reading schedule, and their peers provide most of the information students need to succeed. If students come to you after an absence, first ask them if they have read the posted reading schedule and/or have spoken with a peer. If they still need help after taking these steps, feel free to provide it. You can answer a quick question in class. For a longer explanation, invite the student to see you during homeroom, lunchtime, or recess.

Running like Clockwork

One of the biggest challenges of implementing a guided reading program in the middle grades is working within the time constraints. Efficiency is essential, and students are among our best assets as we strive to streamline classroom procedures. In addition to helping each other catch up after absences, students can contribute to the smooth functioning of the class by taking responsibility for distributing and collecting the books at the beginning and end of each period.

To get the class started on time, students should be ready to go when the bell rings. Students are asked to read the daily assignment (which includes a list of required materials) as soon as they enter the classroom and then start reading their self-selected or group book. While they read, take care of any issues that may arise (a student who needs attention for whatever reason; a hallway conversation with a colleague that takes a little longer than expected) without having to continually refocus the class. Also, tell students that if a teacher doesn't show up, they should be reading quietly the whole time. Through repetition of classroom practices, students will learn your expectations and meet them.

Book Management Routines

Each student needs a book for group reading. Without a good system for distributing the books at the beginning of the class and collecting them at the end, valuable instructional time can be lost. Set aside a small table in a corner of the classroom for the book repository. At the beginning of the class, the students select the appropriate books and move to their group for silent reading. Minimal problems occur during this part of the procedure, but returning the books is a different matter. When Mark first started this process, he would try to wrap up instruction five minutes early, tell the students to return the books to the table, count the books, and then fuss at the students who hadn't returned their copies. This would often go on until the bell sounded, at which point the students would be anxious to leave and Mark would be anxious to find the books—not the best mood for ending a class. In addition, while five minutes a day for a book roundup might not sound like much, it represents 10 percent of a typical period and is too much time to waste.

The solution is to put the students in charge. Let them be responsible for gathering the books, counting them, and ensuring that they have all been returned. Even if they are reticent at first, eventually they will be motivated to help and work together to ensure all the books are returned every day.

Students occasionally may need to check out copies, particularly if they have missed some class time. There are three possible ways to deal with this:

- Work with the school librarian to set aside a minimum number of the selected titles for the time that the unit is being taught. The librarian is usually happy to help because it increases book circulation.

- Have your own "reserve" copies. For some titles, we have managed to collect enough spare copies through used book sales, books earned as payment from local book fairs, and trading with other teachers. We keep these books in the classroom for emergency use.

- Offer a book from your classroom teaching set. This solution is the least desirable because of occasions when the student forgets to bring the book back to class or is absent.

In all cases, we strongly recommend that you keep close tabs on these books. To keep track of books that are loaned to students, we keep a record on the classroom board—the title of the book, the name of the student who borrowed it, and the date it was taken out. Whatever system you use, find some public method of recording which books are in circulation. With all the things you have to manage in your classroom, it is difficult and impractical to keep track of these books in your head.

Self-selected Reading Books

Self-selected reading (SR) books are vital to sustaining the synergy of the classroom. The students are always working at different paces and on different assignments. Some will finish their work earlier than others. At this point the SR book becomes an important tool in classroom management. Students are expected to read their SR books when they complete their work which includes the group reading assignment, the reader's notebook responses, and the written portion of the weekly assignment. As we say many times at the beginning of and throughout the year, "You are never done...you can always read."

This protocol serves a dual purpose. Students become better readers by reading frequently and they also develop stronger work habits. As every middle school teacher knows, some students will hurry through work to "complete" it so that they can move on to other things. They lack stamina and perseverance. Sloppy, rushed, and casual assignments fly off their desks faster than we can replace them. With the guided reading model, students don't hurry as much. They learn to pace their work because they always have something to do. They discover that there's no point in rushing through a reading assignment, because once they complete it they must read something else. Having an SR book at hand serves to motivate some students and minimize distractions for others.

Using the Library

We strongly believe in developing a classroom library so that students can explore a variety of literary genres and interests. The classroom library is an alternative resource when you can't schedule a formal visit to the school or public library, and when you can't supervise students coming and going from the classroom. It can be a ready resource for students who forget their SR books or for those who are ready to select a new one. When students repeatedly "forget" their SR books, we step in. Usually after we repeatedly select a book from our classroom library for them, their memories will miraculously improve. Again, even reluctant readers will stay on task if given time to read and no other options. Boredom, or the threat of reading a title that is boring, will lead students to select books that are interesting to them.

We recommend scheduling a formal visit to the school library at least every other week so students can select an SR book to take home. Librarians can help students locate engaging texts to read, as well as teach them how to use print and online resources for research. One of the main goals of the guided reading program is creating authentic reading experiences for students so they become life-long readers. Librarians play an integral part in this dynamic process. They are allies in our effort to develop intellectually robust reading units.

Building a Library Collection

Initially, we stocked our classroom library with books we purchased at a used book sale conducted by a local college alumni association. We spent about $80 for 14 grocery bags full of books. The titles were diverse enough to capture the interest of all of our students. Used book sales sponsored by public libraries usually offer books for about 25 cents apiece. The key is not to be too discriminating at first. When you have 150 students reading between a third and eleventh grade level, coming through your classroom every day, you can use almost any young adult book that has appropriate content.

Another great way to get free books is to run a book club (a task parents will sometimes offer to do for you). This is a win/win/win situation for you, your students, and your curriculum. By making low-cost books available to your students, you are encouraging them to read. By accumulating bonus points that you can use to obtain other free books for your classroom, you are building your library. And if the books you are using for your guided reading groups are available from the book club, you can actually acquire resources for your core curriculum.

You can also ask for donations for your class library. Many times your avid readers (and their parents) will be happy to clear shelf space by contributing books they read years ago. Conveniently, less-enthusiastic readers find that these books fit their needs. If you have acquired bonus points from book clubs, you can also reward the students who bring in books; for example, 10 used books can be exchanged for one new book. One year, we gave additional rewards to the students and class who contributed the most books. This approach worked so well that we actually had too many books to store in our libraries. As it turned out, we decided to keep the excess to replenish the stock depleted because of a 10–15 percent annual attrition.

Schedules for Guided Reading Meetings

How can a teacher manage to meet with students in small groups, assess, and grade the progress of 140 or more students, and still manage to teach mini-lessons? Figure 5.2 (on the next page) describes a sample organizational schedule. In this model, the students spend a significant amount of time reading. This time is crucial to improving their reading skills and key to making the guided reading program manageable. Additionally, using silent reading time provides time for the teacher to grade formative assessments, meet with students individually, and balance the pacing of the different classes and groups.

Many facets of this program have been long established as best practices, and these have been adapted to specifically meet the needs of adolescent readers. Where literature circles may work well in high school, many middle school students need more direct teacher involvement to keep them focused. In middle school, silent reading time is not the same as the elementary model of "SSR." During the silent reading described in this book, the expectation is that the student is actively practicing the skill featured in the mini-lesson. In guided reading meetings and in talking to students individually, you will assess students' individual comprehension needs and use the information to guide the creation of your next lesson that will lead them to a higher comprehension level. Vocabulary study, which can be staid and traditional with a list of words unrelated to the student, comes alive as students learn challenging words that relate directly to a book they care about and that they have selected.

Notice in the following sample schedule that you will be meeting with groups only three days a week and conducting mini-lessons on two or three days.

Fig. 5.2. Sample Guided Reading Schedule for the Teacher

Day	Teacher Actions
Monday	**Mini-lesson: Learning the Genre Characteristics** • Students read a short story and brainstorm to identify the attributes of the specified genre • Teacher distributes the guided reading books • Teacher meets with two to three guided reading groups
Tuesday	• Teacher meets with the rest of the guided reading groups to quickly introduce the novel and assign pages to be read • Teacher also assigns something for students to think about and write about in their journals for the next meeting
Wednesday	**Mini-lesson: What Is Rising Action?** • Silent reading for whole group • Whole group share: Identify the rising action in your story. How does it build tension in your story?
Thursday	**Mini-lesson: Check in with students and revisit rising action mini-lesson** • Whole group reads guided reading books silently • Meet with two or three guided reading groups and assign new pages to read as well as a new reader's notebook entry
Friday	• Whole group reads silently and completes guided reading assignment • Meet with individual students as needed

There is significant time on Wednesdays and Fridays to plan future group meetings, document grades from guided reading groups, determine which mini-lessons to teach, and meet informally with students one on one. The guided reading group meetings are demanding, but they are not an all-day, every-day proposition. Build time in the schedule to reflect about the group meetings with the students and making adjustments. This task is best done during class time, when the experience is fresh. If you wait until the end of the week, or even the end of the day, the insights will tend to blur together.

Within the guided reading model, students have a schedule to follow. Figure 5.3 on the next page shows a version of one week of activities.

Fig. 5.3. Sample Guided Reading Schedule for Students

Day	Class Work	Homework
Monday	• Mini-lesson (10 minutes) • Guided reading group meeting (15 minutes) • Silent reading of guided reading or self-selected reading book (25 minutes)	Read self-selected reading book (30 minutes)
Tuesday	• Silent reading (35 minutes) • Written response to guided reading meeting assignment (15 minutes)	
Wednesday	• Mini-lesson (10 minutes) • Silent reading: self-selected reading book or guided reading book (30 minutes) • Reader's notebook writing assignment (10 minutes) • Participate in a whole-group share (5 minutes)	Group book reading (10–30 minutes)
Thursday	• Whole-group meeting (15 minutes) • Self-selected reading book writing assignment (25 minutes) • Group share (10 minutes)	Write about how the setting contributes to the mood of the story in reader's notebook (15 minutes)
Friday	• Silent reading of guided reading group book (35 minutes) • Writing in response to guided reading (15 minutes)	

In summary, the weekly time allocation for the sample guided reading schedule has students:

- Reading silently for two hours and ten minutes or more each week.

- Writing in response to their reading for at least one hour.

- Participating in a guided reading discussion for 30 minutes.

The amount of reading that students do in the guided reading program exceeds that in a traditional language arts curriculum, where the focus is on teacher lecture and whole-group instruction.

Guided Reading in Perspective

Although many aspects of the guided reading unit are managed by the teacher, students also have responsibility for maintaining the flow of work in the program. The teacher sets the framework, establishes the routines, and guides the students as they engage in the process of guided reading. At any given moment, students may choose to read a self-selected text, work on a group reading assignment, or read the group book. They are responsible and accountable for meeting deadlines with minimal supervision. Multiple opportunities are provided for students to express their opinions about the texts they are reading either in writing, in a small group setting, or in a whole group share. Furthermore, they spend a very limited amount of time listening to the teacher lecture or even listening to other students in a whole group setting. The majority of their time is spent reading, discussing their thinking about the reading in a small-group setting, or documenting their thinking.

Everything that teachers do to create consistency and eliminate chaos is designed to maximize the time students have to read, write, and reflect. It is impossible to control every student every minute of the day, but a strong classroom culture and structure can support these endeavors. Craft these conditions at the start of the school year to build the foundation for success throughout the year.

Of course, it is sometimes difficult to find time to step back and analyze what is happening in the classroom over the course of a week or even longer. However, by reviewing plan books, checking the schedules posted for the students, and regularly looking at the students' reading journals, you keep a perspective on the way in which the program is meeting students' needs. Below, read about the findings of a student teacher who followed the activities of one of Mark's students for a week to see the variety of tasks in which the student was engaged.

Observing a Student in Mark's Guided Reading Program

A student teacher working in my classroom approached me with an assignment. The student teacher said, "I've been asked by my professor to follow a student for a week. To sort of see what they see from their eyes. I mean, I don't actually follow them. I'm just supposed to watch them and write down what they do." I thought this was a great idea. I had been working on putting together the reading program and had been rolling out the pieces, but had never stopped to really analyze what the week for a student would look like. Was it varied enough, would it be too confusing? Would the students really read when they were supposed to? I added a couple of ideas to the assignment, and the project was on.

The student teacher decided to follow Jake, a gregarious seventh grader. On Monday, Jake's class began with a mini-lesson. This lesson was followed by a writing assignment that he worked on during his 25 minutes of reading time that followed. The last part of the day was spent in a relatively short guided reading group.

Tuesday's class started with a long stretch of time (30 minutes) where Jake was able to work on the previous day's group reading assignment. He spent most of this time reading and during the last 10–15 minutes, he put together his notes to get ready for the next meeting. When the student teacher asked how this day went, Jake responded, "I was glad to have time to finish all that work. I was really glad I could just read and not listen to the teacher today."

Wednesday, Jake was not so lucky; he had to listen to the teacher, but only for 10 minutes, as I gave a lesson on setting. The rest of the time he got to focus on his self-selected reading book, making an entry on the setting in his reader's notebook. The class wrapped up with five minutes of whole-group sharing, something that Jake noted, "was kind of fun to do after being quiet for a lot of the hour."

Thursday was a lot more active for Jake; he started with a group meeting (it went a little long due to the interest of the group), followed by an SR reading and a written assignment that took most of the rest of the hour. He only had a few minutes to read on this day before it was time for group sharing.

On Friday, Jake had most of the hour to work on his reading assignment from Thursday and to make notes about the questions I had asked the group to consider. In all, this day was a day of focused reading for Jake.

In looking back over the student teacher's notes, I was glad to see that there was a diversity of assignments and tasks, and although Jake was expected to read silently for long periods of time, this was broken up by both small-group and whole-group instruction, something important for a social student like Jake.

Reflections on Adolescent Literacy

Read the quote below and then answer the questions on the following page:

"Teachers play a crucial role in supporting, facilitating, and guiding productive group work. Although teachers need to manage the learning environment—including noise level, student movement, and material distribution—that's not enough. They also need to monitor and adjust the other quality indicators. Are students interacting in meaningful ways, as shown by their verbal interactions? Do you see joint attention to tasks and materials?" (Frey, Fisher, and Everlove 2010).

1. What routines have you implemented in your classroom to ensure that students are productive when working in groups?

2. What advice would you give a colleague who wants to implement the type of group work described in the guided reading model?

3. In the guided reading model, students read silently for two hours and ten minutes or more each week. How does the amount of time your students spend reading silently compare to the allocation in the guided reading model?

4. What activities do you use to become informed about the quality of your students' silent reading experiences?

Enhancing Reading through Vocabulary Study and Writing

Chapter 6

In the Classroom with *Julie*

As I stand outside my door monitoring the hallway between classes, Izzy, a friendly student who is always full of questions, approaches me.

Izzy: Mrs. Donnelly, Caitlyn said we're having a test today. How can we have a test over the book? We all read different books, so you can't give us the same test. Are we going to answer questions about the book? Because I didn't study. That's not really fair.

Julie: Izzy, did you make notes when you read?

Izzy: Yeah.

Julie: Did you read the book?

Izzy: Yeah.

Julie: I know you paid attention during the meetings, so you'll be okay.

Izzy: (*yelling over her shoulder as she entered the classroom*) Fine, Mrs. Donnelly. But I hate tests.

A few minutes later I put Izzy's fears and those of her classmates to rest when I gave the assignment.

Julie: Good morning, everyone. We just finished our adventure genre study and you have read one guided reading book and one self-selected novel. For your test, you will be required to write a paper that compares the two stories. We will focus on the aspects that we discussed in our mini-lessons as well as those concepts that we discussed in our guided reading meetings together. For this paper, you can use your novels and your guided reading notes. You will have two class periods to complete this paper and I will provide you with a specific outline of questions for the guided reading novel you each read. This is a test, so I will not answer specific questions for you, but I will be able to help you with writing conventions and give advice on how to edit your paper.

Here's an example of the kind of question that may appear on your essay test:

During our adventure unit, our guided reading focused on how the main character had to "survive" in an unfamiliar or dangerous setting. Think about your guided reading book. Ask yourself, "What was the setting like?" For instance, in *Touching Spirit Bear*, Cole had to survive on an uninhabited island for a year as part of his punishment for a crime. What was dangerous about the setting? Describe the setting and write about the challenges Cole faced. Then compare *Touching Spirit Bear* to the novel you chose to read. Describe the setting in your self-selected adventure book. How was it dangerous or unfamiliar to the main character? How was it similar to your guided reading novel? How did the setting differ? What did the main character have to do to survive? Okay, let's get started. Select the sheet that has the name of your guided reading novel on it and you can begin to write.

As the class began to work, Izzy's hand made its way toward the ceiling.

Julie: Yes, Izzy. What is it?

Izzy: (*with a smile*) Mrs. Donnelly, I see what you mean about how I didn't have to worry. We've already talked about these things in the group meetings, and I made some great notes. I'm good at that. This test will be a piece of cake. All I have to do is write what I already know.

Julie: Don't be overconfident. You've still got to do the work, but I'm sure you'll do great.

Because students have already done all of the hard work by thinking about the topics in the guided reading meetings, this paper should not be something that is daunting to them. In fact, students love the idea that they can look at their guided reading notes and novels to get evidence to support their thinking.

The guided reading model enables middle grade teachers to support students in the broader dimensions of literacy, not just reading. The small group meetings are great for developing students' speaking and listening skills. Structured vocabulary lessons based on the guided reading and self-selected books build students' knowledge of the correct meaning, spelling, and use of words in spoken and written language (Allen 2007). Writing notes and reflections in the reader's notebooks further expands their skills of analysis and communication. The writing activities included in the guided reading model supplement the broader writing curriculum—they are not intended to be a substitute for that curriculum.

Making Vocabulary Study Realistic

Words matter, whether in talking, listening, reading, writing, or learning. Our students need to realize the importance and value of words in their lives. We want them to become "verbivores." If you are a *verbivore*, it is likely that your students will begin to develop the same affinity for words. We often tell our students that when we read, and come to an unfamiliar word, we read "around" the text to figure out the general meaning based on the context. This gives us clues to what the word means and we continue reading. Adult readers don't necessarily stop at every unfamiliar word and look it up in the dictionary. Many times, we will ask another person for help in deciphering the word and have a short conversation about it until we decide on the correct meaning. In your guided reading groups, try to emulate real-life reading experiences by following the same protocol. When students come to an unfamiliar word in their text, provide them with a description or example, much like what we would provide to a friend who asked what a term or phrase meant.

However, developing students' vocabularies requires more than emulating the actions of mature adult readers. "Vocabulary knowledge is so instrumental to reading comprehension—and to overall success in school—that it must receive focused and deliberate attention across the curriculum and throughout the school day" (Yopp and Yopp 2007). Comprehension, fluency, and achievement are all affected by vocabulary knowledge. Guided reading provides many opportunities for students to build their vocabularies. Wide reading is an important means of acquiring new words and students in our classes do a lot of reading. They read the novels we select for instruction and they self-select books for their independent reading. They talk about the books in the guided reading meetings, exchanging ideas about story events, characters, setting, and words that intrigue them. The guided reading experience directly supports acquisition of vocabulary by providing a context for unfamiliar words. When students question the meaning of a word, they can search for clues through a character, scene, or dialogue from books they are already invested in. This background knowledge supports their attempts to establish meaning for the word. Similarly, this engagement with text contributes to effective comprehension, an active process in which the reader integrates prior knowledge with text information and word meaning to gain new knowledge (Pressley 2002; Bromley 2007). Creating a setting in which students have opportunities to come to their own conclusions about a concept or the meaning of a word provides for more solid understanding. Learning is an active process in which learners should discover principles, concepts, and facts for themselves; consequently, it is important to encourage guesswork and intuitive thinking as part of developing word consciousness (Graves and Watts-Taffe 2002).

Building the Word Wall

To help students construct meaning from the texts they read, we ask them to choose their own vocabulary words from the books used in guided reading. Students will learn best when they are engaged, so we don't want to dictate a random list of words that are disconnected from their reading. Again, we know that most middle school teachers are responsible for 120–150 students and that the thought of every student choosing an entry for the word wall might seem overwhelming. Rest assured; you only need one display for each grade level. Because each of us teaches more than 120 students at a time, we treat vocabulary development as a joint project for all of our classes.

Unfamiliar words students find in their texts may become word wall entries. Through these public displays of words that support teaching and learning, we can spend time exploring,

Julie led a brief conversation about the importance of determining meaning through context clues. A student read aloud a sentence where the word *pugnacious* appeared. One of the students shouted out, "It has something to do with a dog, like a pug, the ones with the squashed faces." Another student said she owned a pug dog that was really confrontational. It never backed down from a challenge. We decided the word was synonymous to fighting or arguing. *Pugnacious* became a topic of conversation. Students would recount if someone had been pugnacious in the hall. The students took a word from their text and brought it into their world.

discussing, and using new terms—key strategies for acquiring vocabulary (Cunningham and Allington 1994). These words are ones that you would like your students to use in conversations, and in their writing throughout the year (Allen 2007). The word wall can be displayed on a whiteboard, blackboard, butcher paper or any other open space in a classroom. Figure 6.1 is an example of a word wall typical of what we develop with our students.

Fig. 6.1. A Typical Word Wall

To guide students in the selection of word wall entries, Julie begins the year with a mini-lesson. She reads aloud a short piece of engaging text while simultaneously displaying it on an overhead projector. As she reads, she asks her students to identify a word that they think every student their age should know. For each recommendation, the class discusses reasons for including the word on the list. Julie points out the descriptive qualities of the word and identifies the part of speech. She facilitates a short discussion about the specific and descriptive qualities of the word. By the time class ends, students have a solid understanding of what makes a word worthy of deep understanding and further study.

In this example from an eighth grade class, Julie is leading a discussion about a short story, "Only a Dollar's Worth" (Werner 1993). The main character is an elderly man who drives every day to the same gas station where he buys only a dollar's worth of gasoline for his car. The man is often very rude to the gas station attendant named Isabelle, who later learns to look past the customer's grumpiness and realizes that he is a sad person on a fixed income. After Julie finished reading this story, she asked the class for recommendations for words to include on the word wall.

Ben: I think *frugal* is a good word for the word wall.

Julie: I agree. What do you think *frugal* means?

Ben: (*considered for a moment*) I think it means to be cheap and penny-pinching because Mr. Watts acts like a cheapskate by only buying one dollar's worth of gas and expecting Isabelle to check the oil and wash the windows, too.

Julie: It is similar to those words, but it has a more specific meaning. Who else has an idea of what *frugal* means?

Christina: *Frugal* seems like more of a positive word than the word *cheap*. I think it's more like the word *thrifty*.

Julie: (*probing for more nuance*) What does *thrifty* mean?

Christina: I thought *thrifty* meant to be sensible with money.

Julie: How is *thrifty* different or similar to the word *cheap*?

Johnny: Both words, *thrifty* and *frugal*, sound like positive words. My mom cuts out coupons, but she is not acting cheap. I think my mom is frugal, but she's not a cheapskate.

Julie: I like the way you're thinking about this word. *Frugal* is a very specific and descriptive word that means to be careful with one's money. The word *thrifty* is an excellent synonym for *frugal*. I will place *frugal* on our word wall so you can see it and remember to use it.

As the conversation shows, students benefit from vocabulary study where they select words that are meaningful to them and discuss and reflect on the words. Julie didn't tell the students what to do. Ben selected a word and Julie prompted him to think about it. She asked why he selected the word and what he thought it meant. Julie reinforced a classroom culture that supports word study and put students in charge of selecting, talking, and thinking about vocabulary.

Getting Everyone on Board

What if students choose not to participate in the word wall selection process? Don't worry; they usually come around eventually. Some students hesitate until they realize that they will be tested on the words chosen by their classmates. They decide they might as well have a say in what they will study. By the end of the year, most students will have contributed at least two words to the word wall. Ask students to write their word selections in their reader's notebooks and share them in guided reading meetings. Julie sometimes asks her students to write down their words on a sticky note and place the notes in a bin on her desk so that the words can be readily accessed at an appropriate time. This practice is consistent with the process that Marzano (2003) recommends for students as they read their self-selected books. Allen (2007) recommends that new words should be added to the word wall as they are encountered to ensure that this feature is a vital part of the classroom.

"Knowing a word is not an all-or-nothing proposition; there are gradations of word knowledge that range from no knowledge to rich decontextualized knowledge of a word, including its relationship to other words and its extension to metaphorical uses."

(Beck and McKeown 1991)

In addition to having students provide words for the word wall, we use other activities that encourage them to explore new words. We provide them with a worksheet on which they can record unfamiliar words, suggest a definition, and provide an illustration for the word. Another form is used to have students identify words or phrases from the context that provide a clue to the meaning of the unfamiliar word and to provide a logical guess about the meaning of the word. (See Appendix B for examples of student word study thinking sheets.) Ask students to provide a description, rather than a definition, of the word—a useful practice in direct instruction for vocabulary that is essential for understanding important concepts. These activities involve students in elaborating on the meanings of new words rather than looking up definitions in the dictionary or memorizing definitions for a prescribed set of words (Marzano 2004).

Writing in the Guided Reading Classroom

Be mindful of the need to use language to communicate and express understanding. Writing and reading are interdependent. When students write about a text they have read, their comprehension is enhanced because the writing provides "students with a tool for visibly and permanently recording, connecting, analyzing, personalizing, and manipulating key ideas in the text" (Graham and Herbert 2010). Guided reading in the middle grades presents three distinctly different but important writing opportunities.

Note-Taking

Chapter 5 explained the use of notebooks exclusively for guided reading group meetings. When Mark first started using this method, he created questions, typed them, copied them, and distributed them to the students. Preparing and printing questions for six groups that were reading three or more books and meeting six or seven times each—well, let's just say he soon became wiser about how to spend his time.

After a conversation with a colleague from the science department about the need to improve students' note-taking skills, Mark realized that students should learn how to write the guided reading questions on their own. This became an opportunity for them to practice taking notes while a teacher is talking. The small group environment supports the development of this skill. To start, Mark states the questions and gives the students limited time to write the questions in their notebooks. They can ask for clarification without being fearful of sounding stupid in front of a larger group. Students use the notes to help them respond to prompts the teacher assigns for the next group meeting. The notes are used as part of the grading process to encourage the students to document their thinking. This practice reinforces note-taking skills students are learning in other classes.

"To take effective notes, a student must make a determination as to what is most important, and then state that information in a parsimonious form. ... Although we sometimes refer to summarizing and note-taking as mere 'study skills,' they are two of the most powerful skills students can cultivate. They provide students with tools for identifying and understanding the most important aspects of what they are learning."

(Marzano, Pickering, and Pollock 2001)

Writing to Support Comprehension

Reading response essays integrate the self-selected and guided group texts by examining common genre characteristics. These essays supplement the required writing curriculum and include persuasive essays, personal narrative essays, and a research paper, all of which are required by our state standards. Have students write response essays at the end of a guided reading unit. Or, give the entire class the same writing prompt that requires them to draw upon the guided reading book and the self-selected books. For example, if you taught a mini-lesson on the techniques authors use to indicate the passage of time in books, ask the students to compare the methods and cite relevant passages in their guided reading and self-selected reading books. Figure 6.2 illustrates the work that one student generated.

Fig. 6.2. A Partial Student Response Letter Regarding the Book,
***Make Lemonade* by Virginia Euwer Wolff (1993)**

The phrase, "When life gives you lemons, make lemonade," means that when in life you are given hard things, and put in hard situations (lemons), you should take the bad things and turn them into something good, like lemonade.

Having lemons literally is not so great. They are hard, sour, and impossible to eat by themselves. But with a little creativity, you can take those sour lemons and turn them into something good, like lemonade.

In the book Make Lemonade, Jolly takes her lemons and turns them into lemonade on page 91, when she and LaVaughn walk through the halls and she "shimmies her shimmy of 'I ain't got no problems, no babies dat disappeared on me," she makes the best out of a bad situation and is able to dance and laugh.

Another example is on pages 35 and 67. Jolly is recovering from the nasty incident that happened at work, but still she refuses to sit and wallow in her own misery. She calls the secretary 11 times in 3 days, demanding that she talk to her boss. In this case, she hasn't truly made lemonade yet.

The student expands on the theme and in this case, also the title of the book, while providing explicit evidence to support her analysis of the main character, Jolly. The letter provides an opportunity for students to demonstrate the quality of their understanding. The response letter serves as an assessment of student comprehension while also providing students practice in analytical writing.

The student reader's notebook is another useful source to assess the students' comprehension and mastery of curriculum standards.

Fig.6.3. Excerpt from a Student's Reader's Notebook

In Crossing Jordan, I noticed there was something symbolic in the name of the girl's running team called "Chocolate Milk." Both chocolate and milk are good by themselves, but when you mix them, they're even better. This could mean that the girls, one being African-American and one being Caucasian, are better together as a team than they are alone.

When Julie examined Claire's work (shown in figure 6.3), she noticed that the student understood the grade-level appropriate text and she was beginning to understand many dimensions of the human experience. She was applying the reading strategies of connecting, predicting, and inferring.

Another way to encourage writing is to create a series of essay prompts specific to each book and let students select the question(s) they would like to answer. Allowing students to use their notes for this assignment will reinforce the importance of note-taking during the group meetings.

A third possibility is creating a standard essay test where the students are required to write the paper in a set time period with no assistance from the teacher. This is good practice for writing in the test genre in other classes and on standardized tests.

Home Connections

One of the most beneficial and informative meetings Julie has ever had was when she invited the district's literacy coordinator into her classroom to observe her teaching a guided reading meeting. After a short coaching session, the coordinator offered her some useful advice on how to help students practice their literacy skills at home and make connections to the classroom lessons. He suggested a 30-minute reading assignment followed by a writing assignment drawn from the reading. The writing assignment could be framed around reading strategies, author's craft, story elements, or other concepts the students have been taught throughout the year. If you're worried about reluctant readers, a parent signature might go a long way in helping students remember to finish their home reading assignment.

Give homework that includes reading a self-selected reading book for 30 minutes and writing two to three paragraphs of reflection. Julie has her students read their self-selected reading two to three times a week at home. She may ask them to write a response to such questions as, "What struck you as you read about the setting of your book?" or, "How does the author of your book use dialect to inform the reader about the cultural aspects of the setting?" The students write their responses in the reader's notebook. These writing samples can be used in various ways: formally assessed to determine a grade, as a quick "check-in" to see how an individual student is progressing, or as catalysts for a whole group share session to reinforce the mini-lesson of the previous day.

Students have many opportunities to write in the guided reading program. They can write notes, personal reflections, answers to questions, or essays. The group books provide a significant resource for the students to write engaging pieces on a literary topic that they have become familiar with throughout the guided reading study.

Reflections on Adolescent Literacy

Read the quotations below and answer the following questions.

"The literature on vocabulary development emphasizes three primary means of enhancing students' vocabulary: wide reading, explicit instruction of words and word-learning strategies, and the establishment of an environment that promotes word consciousness" (Yopp and Yopp 2007).

1. What instructional practices do you use to enhance students' vocabularies?

2. What features of your classroom environment promote word consciousness?

"When kids write about those things that matter to them, they do write and they do read, thoughtfully and thoroughly. Through giving kids choices as they read and write, we also teach them to take responsibility for their own learning" (Rief 2003).

3. What kinds of writing experiences do you provide for your students?

4. How do you balance the need to fulfill the mandated curriculum standards and the need to provide students choices in what they read and write?

Establishing Reading Goals through Mini-lessons

Chapter 7

In the Classroom with *Julie*

Early in the school year I teach a mini-lesson about the techniques authors use to introduce characters to their readers. The mini-lesson gives students a foothold for exploring character analysis in greater depth, particularly understanding how a character's actions move the plot forward. The mini-lesson is just the first in a series of steps leading back and forth to the state standard focusing on the role of antagonists and protagonists in literature, as well as internal and external conflicts that authors reveal through character details. A sample mini-lesson is described.

Julie: I am going to read a passage to you from one of my favorite books and I would like you to pay attention to the character named Kenny.

I read a section of Chapter 1 of *The Watsons Go to Birmingham—1963*, where a character named Byron, while scraping the ice off the windows of the car in freezing weather, gets his lips stuck to the side-view mirror of the car because he was trying to kiss himself. His younger brother, Kenny, could have left Byron stuck there as retribution for the awful tricks Byron had played on him over the years. Instead, Kenny immediately sought his parents' help.

Julie: Based on this passage, what can you say about Kenny?

John: I think Kenny is a very forgiving person. If that were my brother, I would have left him stuck to the mirror and made fun of him.

Julie: What does the author do to help you understand Kenny's personality?

Shivani: The author wrote about what Byron did to Kenny and how he tricked Kenny and then showed us what Kenny was thinking when Byron got stuck.

I silently note that Shivani has demonstrated an understanding of how the author used inner dialogue to reveal character traits.

Julie: You're right, the author told about Byron's actions, which gave us insight to Byron. He let us into Kenny's head. We call this *inner dialogue*. By knowing how Byron acted and what Kenny was thinking, we learned about Kenny. So how does this help us understand the story better as we move forward?

Samantha: I think Byron is a troublemaker and will be a problem for Kenny throughout the story. I think the story might be about how Kenny deals with his older brother's bad behavior and learns from it.

Here I note that Samantha has made a prediction. Because this lesson is early in the school year, I decide to directly name the reading strategies that students would use throughout the term.

Julie: Good job, Samantha. That was a great *prediction*. When authors want to introduce characters to their readers, they can do a number of things. Authors may have the main character say something, do something, or think something that gives the readers insight to the character's personality. The author may also tell the reader what other characters think about the main character. All of these things help us understand the main character's personality. By understanding the character's personality, we can then use this character's actions to predict what will happen next in the plot.

Before the students move from the guided reading group to their self-selected readings, I assign a written reflection to link the treatment of character in the group book and their self-selected books. In their reader's notebooks, the students must choose a character from their self-selected books and explain how the author revealed the character's personality through words and actions. Based on their understanding and text examples, the students then would predict what the character might do next in the story. A follow-up mini-lesson might define the terms *protagonist* and *antagonist* and relate them to the guided reading texts.

A mini-lesson is a quick, explicit lesson that focuses on literary concepts or reading comprehension skills (Calkins 1986). The mini-lesson format is useful because it's short, usually five to 10 minutes, and anchors the class to a common goal while they read. The mini-lesson also serves as a nice transition into the guided reading time where students can see how authors use particular techniques such as inner dialogue to relay a character's intentions or introduces a red herring to create a plot twist. Students might notice mood, tension, metaphors, elements of setting, or any of the dozens of different topics that you have chosen to discuss in prior mini-lessons.

Keeping the mini-lesson to the five- to 10-minute time limit may be challenging, but with careful planning you can do it. Remember that you want to have your students reading for the better part of each class period. If you're talking, they're not reading.

A planning sheet for mini-lessons is shown in figure 7.1. This form includes sections for "literary focus" or "literacy strategy focus," two important areas in which explicit instruction is needed for middle grade students. These areas serve to show compliance with language arts curriculum standards. The cumulative plan sheets for a unit are useful in helping evaluate your program offerings to ensure that you are addressing the standards and providing explicit instruction on a regular basis. Sample mini-lessons are provided in Appendix C.

Fig. 7.1. Mini-lesson Plan Sheet

Mini-lesson Planning Form
Lesson Plan Title: _____
Lesson Purpose: _____
Target Students: _____
Literary Focus (curriculum standard): _____
or, Literacy Strategy Focus (curriculum standard): _____
Procedure: _____
_____
_____
Student Activity: _____
_____
_____
Assessment: _____
_____
_____
Example:

Choosing Mini-lessons

In a mini-lesson, the teacher defines the concept or strategy and models its application—the first step in the gradual release of responsibility model. The choice of topics for mini-lessons is based on data from student assessments and the required curriculum standards and benchmarks. Mini-lessons based on topics in these areas will support your selected themes as well as the ongoing needs of your students. A sampling of topics for mini-lessons is shown in the chart on the following page.

Try to teach a five- to 10-minute mini-lesson two to three times a week based on students' needs and the standards required for a particular unit. On the other days, teach a five-minute recap lesson to the whole group. This sequence ensures enough time to meet with at least two guided reading groups during each 55-minute class period and still gather your classes for a three- to five-minute whole group sharing session at the end.

"Throughout a well-structured unit, teachers are continually providing input to students regarding new content. Sometimes this occurs in the form of answers to questions, discussions with individual students, discussions with small groups of students, and other types of rather spontaneous interactions. At other times, input is planned as part of the overall design of the unit. For example, a teacher might plan to have students engage in one or more of the following activities: read a section of the textbook, listen to a lecture, observe a demonstration, be part of a demonstration, or watch a video. I refer to these designed input activities as critical-input experiences."

(Marzano 2007)

Standards-Based Mini-lesson Topics

Literary Focus

- How Literature Reflects Real Life
- Making Connections to Literature
- Literary Genre Characteristics
- Setting
- Mood
- Elements of the Plot
- Point-of-View
- Internal/External Conflicts
- Consistency and Believability of Narration
- Character Perspectives
- Symbolism
- Story Themes
- Foreshadowing
- Flashback
- Figurative Language
- Imagery

Literacy Strategies Focus

- Prediction
- Inference
- Analysis and Synthesis
- Visualization
- Questioning
- Self-monitoring
- Using Context
- Understanding Prefixes, Suffixes, Base Words

Procedural Mini-lessons

Initially, many of your mini-lessons will focus on procedures that will help students understand how to conduct themselves in a guided reading classroom. To build a classroom culture that encourages student participation in guided reading, Julie teaches a mini-lesson about establishing rules for the groups. She asks, "What makes a book discussion productive? What do you think is the purpose of guided reading meetings? What are some of the benefits of talking about a story with your classmates? What sometimes frustrates you during conversations with your classmates?"

She writes her students' responses on a piece of chart paper and uses these to frame the expectations for guided reading conversation expectations. One brainstorming session produced these criteria:

- Be respectful and allow everyone in the group to speak.

- Don't interrupt.

- Really listen to what each person has to say and comment on his or her points.

- Ask questions if you don't understand.

- Turn back to the book if you can't remember something about the story.

- Use page numbers so everyone can follow along.

- Do the assignment and be prepared.

Although students may be able to identify behaviors that contribute to an effective discussion, this does not mean that they easily put these into practice. Have students refer to the criteria periodically as a way of helping them to evaluate their performance in guided reading meetings.

Thematically Linked Mini-lessons

Mini-lessons can also follow weekly themes. Focusing on the same mini-lesson theme throughout the week allows you to introduce an additional topic to extend the learning of advanced readers during their guided group meeting while providing deeper support for struggling readers during their meeting. For example, exploring the concept of point-of-view can range from a simple personal narrative told through the main character's reflections to a more complex structure in which the narrators change, as does the point-of-view throughout the book. To explore the structure in which narrators change, use the book *Seedfolks* (2004) by Newbery Medalist Paul Fleischman about the creation of an urban community garden, and Konigsburg's *A View from Saturday* (1998), another Newbery-honored book about the friendships among students on a sixth grade quiz bowl team. The whole-class mini-lesson could focus on defining point-of-view and identifying the point-of-view in a simple text. Then use the lesson as a launching point for conversations in each of the guided reading groups. A description of this approach to a point-of-view mini-lesson and follow-up in differentiated groups is shown in the text box on page 142.

Point-of-View Mini-lessons

To introduce the lesson you might say, "When authors write a book, someone has to tell the story. Some authors have the main character tell the story by describing personal experiences. A story told in this way is called first-person narrative and the point-of-view is that of the main character. Other authors use a narrator, an all-knowing or omniscient person, who stands apart from the characters but knows a lot about them. A story told by a narrator is called a *third-person narrative*. The narrator's point-of-view is presented in the story. Sometimes an author will use more than one narrator to tell the story. In those stories, it is possible that different narrators will have different ideas or points-of-view about how the story is developing."

After this introduction, place text on an overhead projector and/or read aloud a couple of different texts that feature both first- and third-person narratives. Then discuss the point-of-view in each selection and ask students to identify details that reveal the point-of-view. For example, the use of the pronoun *I* or the presentation of information that goes beyond what the characters would know are details that students might point out.

Next, move to the guided reading group portion of the day. Keep in mind that the mini-lesson is only an introduction to the *terminology* associated with point-of-view. Because of the recursive nature of the language arts standards, you will teach a series of mini-lessons over several weeks to reflect all the shades of this topic.

Point-of-View Lessons in Three Guided Reading Groups

We have used three texts to teach the literary concept of point-of-view at the students' appropriate instructional level. All the students had been introduced to point-of-view in a mini-lesson. In the guided reading meetings, we were able to shape instruction to the needs of the students and the nature of the texts they were reading. The chart on the next page suggests the possibilities for differentiated teaching of point-of-view within the guided reading groups.

Point-of-View Lesson Differentiated Within the Guided Reading Groups

Comprehension Level	Book Title	Lesson Focus
Developing Readers	*Code Talker*	How does the author's point-of-view affect the telling of the story? Do the narrator's individual experiences impact how he sees, describes, and experiences the world? Why did the author choose a narrator with this particular point-of-view?
Grade Level Readers	*Chains*	What is the credibility of the narrator? Are the character's background experiences and emotions represented in her narration of the story and her point-of-view regarding her current situation?
Advanced Readers	*The Watsons Go to Birmingham—1963*	Who is telling this story? How does this person's perspective influence your interpretation of what is happening?

These books provide a great opportunity to delve deeper into the concept of point-of-view. Although the mini-lesson by itself would move the students further along the path of understanding point-of-view, by immediately following up in the group meeting, we are able to reinforce the concepts with texts familiar to the students.

For example, previous lessons for the group reading *Chains* focused on how the main character, Isabel, had come to an agreement with the Patriots based not on her belief in their ideals, but her hope for freedom for herself and her sister. The conversations had prepared the students to deeply think about Isabel's motivations and feelings and to apply this information to their knowledge of point-of-view.

The group reading *Code Talker* had been touching upon the idea that the narrator had a very specific, and somewhat unique, point-of-view. His particular background impacted how he saw the world and interpreted historical events. As the narrator grew and changed, the group was able to use character analysis to examine the writer's thinking by exploring why the author would choose this particular narrator.

With *The Watsons Go to Birmingham—1963* group, we took the technique introduced in the mini-lesson and reinforced it with concrete examples from the group book.

The mini-lesson is an extraordinarily valuable tool at your disposal. By establishing a short time period in which you present important concepts and ideas to students, you can cover a lot of ground in the curriculum without causing students to lose focus as they might during long lectures. Early in the year the mini-lessons can be focused on classroom management. Later, when the class is deep into a guided reading unit, you can use the mini-lessons to introduce literacy strategies and to revisit previously taught lessons on literary concepts. As the unit progresses, you can re-visit these concepts as necessary. The flexibility and adaptability of the mini-lesson makes it a very important piece of the guided reading program.

Reflections on Adolescent Literacy

Read the following quote and answer the questions below.

"Although direct instruction has earned a bad reputation over the years, there is nothing wrong with direct instruction in and of itself. It is the overreliance on direct instruction that inhibits learning. The key is to match your instructional approach to the subject matter and the teaching needs of your students. Direct instruction is an efficient means of helping students learn and can be very effective with helping students acquire certain types of knowledge" (Jackson 2009).

1. For what purposes do you use direct instruction in your classroom?

2. In what ways do you organize lessons to ensure a balance between whole-class direct instruction and small-group or individual instruction?

3. In what ways are the mini-lessons described in this chapter representative of your instructional practices? What are the similarities? What are the differences?

4. The terms *direct instruction* and *explicit instruction* are widely used by educators. How do you use these terms in relation to instruction you provide in your classroom?

5. Do you think that all educators have the same interpretation of these terms?

6. In what ways are mini-lessons examples of both direct instruction and explicit instruction?

The Impact of Guided Reading on Reading Comprehension Scores

Chapter 8

We often struggle with our effectiveness in the classroom. Are we helping students learn? Should we teach in a different way? Are test scores what they could be? Are the assessments valid? Do they truly measure growth? How do we apply best practices in the classroom?

All these questions and more dogged us as we adopted and adapted this guided reading program. For many years, we believed that these practices had been validated in research; therefore, they should work in the classroom. *Should* is the key word. Early on, we had only our in-class assessments and some broad state test data results to guide us. It *felt* like students were moving forward.

We have used specific measurement tools to more accurately and precisely measure student outcomes and to assess this guided reading program objectively. The program has done well. It would be nice if there were affordable, consistent, holistic assessments that could be performed on all students, but this is not presently the case. In absence of this, the first question that must be asked of any program is: Does it show measurable results?

Background of the Results

Data from the day-to-day teaching of typical teachers in the middle grades illustrates the effectiveness of the guided reading program on students' reading comprehension.

The information was obtained from the measurement instruments that were available in two schools where we taught. These instruments were the Scholastic Reading Inventory (Scholastic 2007) and the STAR Reading Computer Adaptive Test (STAR 2007b). Although we took the time to compile these results, the assessment is really nothing different from what teachers produce all the time. We took what we had and used the results to help us understand that what we were doing in guided reading was working.

About the Schools

- **School 1** is situated in a relatively geographically dispersed, semi-rural school district. The population of the school is primarily non-Hispanic whites, an ethnic group that makes up 95 percent of the approximately 1,000 students. Twenty eight percent of the total student population is classified as "economically challenged" while 15 percent of the students are classified as "learning disabled."

- **School 2** serves a medium-sized municipality. It is one of five middle schools in the district. Of the 700 students in this school, 51 percent are non-Hispanic white, 26 percent are Asian, 13 percent are African American, and seven percent are multi-racial. Thirteen percent of the students are classified as "economically disadvantaged" and eight percent are classified as "learning disabled."

The data to support the effectiveness of the guided reading program are based on three sources. The data that are used for the analysis of the results from School 1 were drawn from one co-taught classroom with two different classes. Mark and a teacher trained in special education taught the sixth grade classes. In total, there were 45 students, 15 of whom were identified as learning disabled and classified as special education students. The measurements were taken in the fall and again in the spring.

Two different data sets are presented for School 2. The first set is from Julie's sixth grade class of 29 students whom Mark taught in seventh grade. (Mark changed schools between his work at School 1 that is documented here and his work at School 2.) These 29 students were scheduled with no advance thought to using them in the evaluation of the data. In fact, they were scheduled into the classes before Mark was hired as the teacher. The data used to measure their growth are the reading scores in the fall of the sixth grade year and the reading scores in the fall of the eighth grade year (after the summer break).

The third data set is the most extensive. It is only a one-year measurement, but it includes a total of 306 students: 185 sixth grade students and 121 seventh grade students. School 2 is in the process of implementing the guided reading model in the middle school and these data are reflective of results from classes where the teachers are using it.

The Teachers Involved

Ten middle school teachers have been chosen to fully implement the program and the number is growing every year. If these teachers were gathered together in one site, they would appear a very eclectic group. In age they range from early 30s to early 60s; in personality they vary from introspective to outgoing. Their interactions with students outside the classroom run the spectrum from gregarious, funny, and outgoing to reserved and proper.

The implementation of this program looks different in each classroom. Some teachers are much more free-flowing in the small group discussions, preferring to focus on fewer large conceptual questions. Others are slightly more directive, showing a tendency to be more involved in the discussions. Still others emphasize vocabulary to a greater degree, while some are more heavily involved in discussing students' independent reading.

The unifying, underlying philosophy of all the teachers who have adopted the program is the belief that student needs drive teaching. The teacher who typically allows more free-flowing discussion will become much more directive when the students show that they need support. The focus on vocabulary will be shifted if the students' response letters are not meeting expectations. The idea that the curriculum serves the students, not the other way around, is the common thread of these teachers' philosophy. Their belief that they should be responsive to student needs every day has led them to embrace this program. And that belief, along with the structure of guided reading in the middle school, has led to the success documented in this chapter.

Results for School 1

During the first two years that we were developing the Guided Reading in the Middle School program, Mark worked for two districts. The first district did not have a formalized assessment program. Consequently, he had to rely on informal measurement and the application of best practices to determine the effectiveness of the program on student achievement. His observations from these sources seemed to indicate the program was working; however, there was no real quantitative measure to support these informal assessments.

In the third year, when the program was fully implemented, a colleague who had access to the STAR Reading computer-adaptive reading test offered to share this resource with Mark and conduct the assessments.

The STAR test produces an individual student's grade level reading equivalency score and provides a national percentile rank, which indicates where that student ranks among all other students who have taken the test in that grade at the same point in the school year. Mark administered the STAR test twice during the school year: as a pretest in late September and early October, and as a post-test in May, which was used to measure student growth over the course of the year. The individual student results were compiled and examined to determine class-wide trends.

The results of the program for general education and special education students when measured by the STAR test are shown in the charts below.

STAR Test Results for Sixth Grade General Education Students in School 1

	Pre-test Fall	Post-test Spring	Change
Percentile Rank	42.8	52.4	+9.6
Grade Level Equivalency	5.8	7.6	+1.8

STAR Test Results for Sixth Grade Special Education Students in School 1

	Pre-test Fall	Post-test Spring	Change
Percentile Rank	18.1	18.6	+0.5
Grade Level Equivalency	3.9	4.9	+1.0

"The STAR Reading computer-adaptive reading test and database is an achievement-level progress-monitoring assessment that provides teachers with accurate reading scores for students in grades K–12 in 10 minutes. As a periodic progress-monitoring assessment, STAR Reading serves three purposes for students with at least 100-word sight vocabulary. First, it provides educators with quick and accurate estimates of reading comprehension using students' instructional reading levels. Second, it assesses reading achievement relative to national norms. Third, it provides the means for tracking growth in a consistent manner longitudinally for all students."

(STAR 2007a)

"The STAR Reading assessment measures reading comprehension. It provides information to help teachers tailor instruction, monitor reading growth, and improve students' reading performance."

(STAR 2007b)

The results across both populations show clear growth above what would be expected. Maintaining the percentile rank from the pre-test to the post-test would show average student growth. If the score did not change at all, it would indicate the overall student ranking was unchanged. If the percentile score increased, the result indicated that the student performed better in the post-test than in the pre-test. If the score decreased, the result showed that the student growth was less than the national norm. In brief, an increase in percentile rank indicates greater than average growth, a decrease means less than average growth. No change would mean average growth.

For the general education students, the test results reflect a growth from an average of 42.8 percentile (about seven points below the mid-point) to a 52.4 percentile, a couple of points above mid-point. This result correlates with a grade level equivalency growth from 5.8 to 7.6. As this was a sixth grade class, the average score for a class performing at grade level at the start of the year would be 6.0. These results indicate that the general education group gained almost a two-year growth (1.8) in grade level equivalency. Expected growth would be about one grade level. Also, the average growth in percentile rank was almost 10.

Although the overall growth from the special education students was statistically lower than that of the general education students, in some ways it is actually more impressive. For the special education students, the overall growth in percentile rank was only one-half a percent. Clearly, this does not measure up to the growth of 9.6 percentile points from the general education population. However, the special education students had all been identified with some form of a learning disability. They actually had moderate growth when compared to the overall population, a population made up of students who primarily are not disabled. So, it may be concluded that the students with reading disabilities improved as much as the general population.

The same concept applies to the grade level growth for the special education group. Although the growth was 1.0 years of grade-level equivalency, what we would expect from a typical student, these students came into the class 2.1 grade-level equivalency years behind the average. Since the average for this population was at 3.9 grade level and they were starting sixth grade, they had shown only about two thirds of the average growth over their academic careers (3.9/6.0). Although the growth of one year in grade level would seem to be "average," the data shows that this group's previous growth was significantly below average. The guided reading program allowed these students to grow well above their previous performance levels.

Another interesting fact that this testing illustrated was the extreme diversity of reading levels within a very small population of students. The lowest score on the STAR assessment was a grade-level equivalency of 2.3, a percentile rank of 2, and the highest was a grade-level equivalency of 12.1, a percentile rank of 95. These results underscore one of the reasons this program works: it provides leveled books and opportunities to teach to each student's needs. Clearly, a "one-size-fits-all" text would not be appropriate for a class containing students who are literally reading between the early-elementary and pre-college grade levels.

Reading fluency, indicated as words correct per minute (WCPM), was measured using the Scholastic Five-Minute Reading Assessments (Rasinski and Padak 2005). The results shown in the chart on the following page indicate significant growth in fluency for both general education and special education students. The growth exceeded that which would normally be expected (Rasinski and Padak 2005). We maintain that this improvement in performance is a direct result of providing students with significant amounts of time to read independently in the guided reading program.

Student Fluency Score Growth in School 1

	Pre-test Fall	Post-test Spring	Change
General Education Students	133	164	+24%
Special Education Students	74	96	+30%

"SRI is designed to measure how well readers comprehend literary and expository texts. It measures reading comprehension by focusing on the skills readers use to understand written material samples from various content areas. These skills include referring to details in the passage, drawing conclusions, and making comparisons and generalizations. …[T]he purpose of SRI is to locate the reader on the Lexile Map for Reading. Once a reader has been measured, it is possible to forecast how well the reader will likely comprehend hundreds of thousands of texts that have been analyzed using the Lexile metric."

(Scholastic 2007)

Results for School 2

The district where Julie teaches has a mandatory district-wide reading comprehension assessment program. The Scholastic Reading Inventory (SRI) is the instrument used to evaluate student performance. The SRI measures a student's comprehension level using adaptive questioning.

Although the SRI and STAR assessments examine similar concepts, the results are presented in a different format. The STAR assessment produces a grade level equivalency and a percentile rank for each student; the SRI produces a Lexile. A Lexile is a measure of a student's overall reading comprehension. This measure is also used to rate the readability of a piece of text.

The interesting thing about the SRI is that it provides overlapping ranges of where a student might be expected to score at a particular grade level. For example, sixth grade students typically measure between 665–1000, seventh grade students between 735–1065, and eighth grade students between 805–1100 (Scholastic 2008).

At first glance, SRI may seem less exact than the STAR program; however, it could be argued that the idea of a range as opposed to assigning a particular grade level is a better reflection of the ability of a standardized test to identify a student's reading level when administered only on occasion. By looking at the Lexile proficiency ranges, we can move toward an idea of what growth we should expect from students. The Lexile proficiency ranges and mid-year levels for grades six, seven, and eight are shown below.

Lexile Proficiency Ranges and Mid-year Levels, Grades 6–8

Grade	Lexile Range	Lexile Midpoint
6	665–1000	832
7	735–1065	900
8	805–1100	952

A quick glance at these numbers shows that the expected growth each year from sixth through eighth grades is about 50 to 70 points. In many ways, an individual teacher guiding and measuring student growth over the school year is more important than achieving a particular grade level equivalency. For example, we may actually be successful with a student who leaves the classroom at the end of the year two full grade levels behind, if he came in at the beginning of the year three grade levels behind. Conversely, if we had a student who was a grade level ahead coming into a class but who leaves reading at grade level, we really cannot claim success with that student.

The results for School 2 focus on Lexile growth. In the first year of measurement, Julie was piloting the program with 90 students in sixth grade. These students showed an average growth of 148 Lexile points. The following year the program was fully used by five language arts teachers, with public school teaching experience ranging from three to 30 years. The average Lexile growth for the 304 students was 134 points. Note that the average Lexile growth is typically between 50–70 points. Among these classes, approximately 30 students were taught using the guided reading in the middle school model for two consecutive years. The mean two-year growth for these students, from the start of sixth grade to the end of seventh grade, was 340 Lexile points. In terms of percentile change, the students went from the 46th percentile to the 79th percentile. These results seem to indicate that effects of the guided reading program are cumulative. The program may very well be creating a reading "disposition" in these students. The impact on student achievement appears to be affected not only by what the teachers are doing in the classroom, but also the students are taking their reading habits out of the classroom and into their homes.

Perspectives on Results from School 1 and School 2

The results from School 1 and School 2 are surprisingly similar. In the small sample from School 1, the students grew by an average of 1.8 grade levels, almost twice the expected growth. In School 2, with the larger sample, the mean growth was about 130 points, about twice the expected growth. From the administration of two different assessment systems, we have obtained data that point toward the effectiveness of the guided reading program in improving students' reading comprehension.

What makes these similar results even more striking is that they were achieved in two very different schools. School 2 is racially and ethnically diverse: 26 percent Asian, 13 percent African-American, 7 percent biracial, 3 percent Hispanic, and 16 percent economically disadvantaged. Seventeen different nationalities are represented: not just students of different ethnic backgrounds, but students who were *born* in 17 different countries. Julie's school also serves a university town with a strong focus on education; however, there is a significant portion of students who are adversely affected economically. The population of School 1 is more rural and less diverse. In addition, this school has a significant percentage of students who are economically impacted and a high population of students who are working with a learning disability. The schools where this program has been piloted serve populations that are very different. The teachers teaching the program have varied teaching styles, dispositions, and experience. In both schools and among the teachers, similar use of the Guided Reading in the Middle School program was the constant factor.

Teachers' Perspectives

We wanted to find out what other teachers using the program had experienced. We sought answers to two questions:

- What are your beliefs about literacy instruction for middle school students?

- What have you observed about your experiences using guided reading?

Survey Questions

The teachers we surveyed included a special education teacher, two eighth grade teachers, one seventh grade teacher, and a teacher of sixth and eighth graders.

What are your beliefs about literacy instruction for middle school students?

I believe that literacy is the key element in comprehending all subjects. Reading and writing are essential skills that are not only necessary for students to possess in school, but are also important in other areas such as college admission, college performance, careers, and daily life. In my experience as a special education teacher, middle school students often relate their literacy skills to their self-esteem. Some who struggle with literacy tend to pose classroom behavior problems. Others attempt to silently become invisible, as not to be recognized by staff and students for their lack in literacy skills.

What have you observed about your experiences using guided reading?

Guided reading was one of the first reading programs I took advantage of after coming to Ann Arbor Schools. I literally witnessed students who had little or no interest in reading develop a love for reading as they moved throughout the library looking for their book of choice. The group talks promoted a relaxing environment where students could excitedly express their thoughts about the events of the story. Having specialized reading and writing programs available to our students has enabled me to reduce the special education services needed for some of my students, as well as to remove some students from the special education because of the availability of these literacy programs. Students who used to be confined to special education classes are now allotted the opportunity to be included with the general education population. Strong, creative, student-centered literacy programs are being used in our middle school ELA classes that allow choice, and encourage positive attitudes toward reading with students.

—*Tanisha Brooks, Special Education Teacher, Clague Middle School*

What are your beliefs about literacy instruction for middle school students?

Literacy for middle school students must include a range of media. Electronic media is important and essential, but does not preclude the focused concentration necessary for deeply understanding a book. Guided reading groups are one way to facilitate and assess student understanding of the book. Because of the range, quantity, and rate that media affects us today, students must be able to think critically about the messages contained in this onslaught of information.

What have you observed about your experiences using guided reading?

Although it may appear that reading three books simultaneously with a class is difficult to manage, students and teachers will discover that guided reading groups (GRG) are a useful and relatively easy structure to set up and maintain. GRG allow the teacher to assess who has done the reading and who hasn't: They can't hide from you in a group of five. Most students enjoy the chance to hold small group discussions with the teacher—they are excited about meetings and often passionate in their discussions. I have gotten to know my students better, and can more accurately understand who needs what.

> —*Kirsten Jensen, 8th grade Language Arts Teacher,*
> *Clague Middle School*

What are your beliefs about literacy instruction for middle school students?

I believe literacy instruction for middle school students is critical in developing future generations who read for pleasure and enabling them to utilize information presented in written form. At the middle school level, conversation about text is vitally important to allow students to more thoroughly process and examine the materials that they read.

What have you observed about your experiences using guided reading?

Guided reading is essential to developing readers who think actively and deeply. My students have expressed insights and observations that surprised me with their depth and nuance. I don't know that I could teach effectively *not* utilizing guided reading practices.

> —*Ellen Daniel, 8th grade Language Arts Teacher,*
> *Scarlett Middle School*

What are your beliefs about literacy instruction for middle school students?

I taught elementary school for 20 years, and now middle school for 12. The same fundamental teaching truths apply. The first bulletin board I put up, in my third and fourth grade classroom, highlighted the four literacy areas: Listen, Speak, Read, Write. Each was connected to a central point: THINK. Make sense of what you read. Connect this to your experiences, knowledge, intuition, and insight.

As an elementary teacher I was able to support connections in the curriculum, and in the minds of students. A word list would not only focus on spelling skills, but support the reading curriculum. It also often included vocabulary used in mathematics, science, and social studies units. Lessons would integrate vocabulary in purposeful contextual activities.

Literacy is just as important in middle school, where the focus is on more complex content. Literacy skills are necessary to support understanding in all subject areas. Specialized vocabulary demands support, and dealing with more abstract concepts requires more specific and higher level skills. Various genres of books and other texts demand literacy instruction. Providing students with a variety of literacy skills at middle school—listening, speaking, reading, or writing—allows them to define and apply their understanding of an ever more complex world.

What have you observed about your experiences using guided reading?

The first maxim of teaching is, "Take students where they are, and go from there." When I know what experiences and skills a student possesses, I can use those to bridge to the next step. Miscalculate, and the student is likely to be bored or befuddled. As often as educational pedagogy goes in cycles, this truism has always been recognized in reading instruction, with attention to appropriate selection of text and awareness of frustration, instructional, and independent reading levels. Given this, guided reading's first goal is to work with books that are at an appropriate level for each student.

The guided reading process promotes active and purposeful practice of all four facets of literacy—reading, writing, listening, and speaking. Lessons support the full range of cognitive development, from vocabulary development, to language conventions, to complex literary analysis. Students are encouraged to dig deeply and communicate effectively, both in group discussions and journal writing. Properly done, the text is read three times: A first reading for broad understanding, a second for analysis and interpretation, and a third reading of key sections to underscore points during the discussion and writing sessions.

Learning to converse, both within the group and with the author, comes from asking probing questions, and brings the text alive. For example, rather than ask, "Why did the 14 year-old girl take care of the 17 year-old?" propose, "Why did the author choose to have a 14 year-old take care of a 17 year-old?" This change of perspective helps the student look at reading, and writing, as an active process, one that both the author and reader must wrestle with to understand on many levels.

Perhaps the strongest asset in guided reading is that the group is small and intimate enough to ensure personal attention to, and participation by, each student. Working with a whole class, the teacher must select objectives and instructional strategies that meet the norm. By doing so, students most in need of targeted skills often lose out. But with a small group, teachers can respond to the needs of each student, while having sufficient conversations that allow the group to gather momentum. Even when I have worked with two groups covering the same text, the dynamics and discussions in each are unique, as the needs, strengths and interests of each student are responded to. Of course, with books selected for the group's instructional reading level, students can focus on appropriate skills and literary interpretation, while still allowing for diverse interests and experiences that are brought to the group. Students have more control, feel more involved, and participate with more meaning.

I have conducted novel discussion groups at both elementary and middle school levels. These tend to be more worthwhile than adult book groups I've attended. Due to the level of focus, individual attention and participation, and higher level thinking skills elicited, guided reading discussions have been among the most powerful learning activities I've participated in during my 33 years of teaching.

—Jeff Gaynor, 7th grade Language Arts and Social Studies Teacher, Clague Middle School

What are your beliefs about literacy instruction for middle school students?

My beliefs for middle school literacy center on structured choice. The choice factor increases every year. I say to my students, "I'll tell you what my instructional goals are and you pick the book from this stack or cart that you want to read." We read, we write, we discuss, and we come to common goals on multiple paths. Everyone loves the experience and everyone learns. It's almost too simple to be believable, but it is exactly what I was looking for.

What have you observed about your experiences using guided reading?

After years of wishing I could teach the *love* of reading instead of reading, I am witnessing the dream. I am watching kids of all levels inhale books and beg for more. I love what I see:

- Sixth grade students thrilled to see the "genre cart" come into the room.

- Reading discussion groups where everyone contributes because they love what they are reading.

- Everyone contributing to a summarizing discussion about the genre characteristics using examples from the text they read to support their point.

Yes! This is the same kind of reading discussion I engage in and enjoy with adult friends over dinner and it's happening on a regular basis in my classroom.

—Linda Prieskorn, 6th and 8th grade Language Arts
and Social Studies Teacher, Clague Middle School

Reflections on Adolescent Literacy

Read the following quote and answer the questions below.

"Determining the work level for students is a little like *Goldilocks and the Three Bears*. You have to find the fit that's just right for your students. If you don't, your story may end with crying children and broken furniture. Ask too little, and the kids are likely to feel patronized or bored. Assignments can seem meaningless to them, no matter what your intention. Ask too much, and many will blame their steady diet of failure on you, the school, the subject, or worst of all, themselves" (Kobrin 2004).

1. In what ways is this quotation representative of the principles and instructional outcomes of guided reading in the middle school?

2. The authors asked teachers who are using the program, "What are your beliefs about literacy instruction for middle school students?" How would you answer this question? How could those beliefs influence the way in which you would implement this program in your classroom?

Guidelines for Developing Guided Reading Units

Chapter 9

In the Classroom with Mark

Like any well-prepared teacher, I spent time planning lessons. I focused on the books the kids were reading, and made detailed notes about what to teach. Each lesson had engaging questions, notes on what might stump the students in a given section, and potential vocabulary words that might be unfamiliar to the students. As I taught my first couple of lessons from the adventure unit, everything was going well. The groups were probing deeply and none were requiring an unusual amount of support. Although I taught five classes and was meeting with 25 groups, most groups were meeting as scheduled and everything seemed to be going very well. However, as any teacher will tell you, this was a sure sign that things were about to go poorly.

The first sign of trouble came during the second hour when a group reading *The Music of Dolphins* (Hesse 1996) couldn't quite grasp how a human girl could view herself as a dolphin. A 15-minute meeting turned into a half an hour. When it became apparent the same class needed additional support on a whole-class assignment that day, the group for the second hour began to fall far behind schedule. "No problem," I thought, "I'll get them caught up tomorrow." Tomorrow featured a fire drill during the second hour. Suddenly, the second-hour groups were far behind the first-hour and third- and fourth-hour groups. Getting off schedule can easily happen if you are not prepared to deal with unanticipated events.

In my planning I had overlooked an important task. I had not been preparing summaries of the chapters for my own use. Suddenly, it became a challenge to recall what was happening in a specific part of the book for the specific lesson being taught. Although I knew the books well, my inability to recall the specifics of a certain section of a book when dealing with groups at two different places proved problematic. The obvious solution was to start to develop summaries of the text to go along with my questions. These brief chapter or section summaries are not designed to replace reading the book, but allow you to quickly shift from one book to another book and quickly "get your bearings." As Julie and I prepared the units, we included chapter summaries with questions designed to support the acquisition of reading strategies, the understanding of story elements, and comprehension traps that may confuse students. The framework that we developed is a model that you can use to develop your own guided reading units. We hope that our guidelines for developing the units will enable you to continually incorporate new books into the mix, keeping the line-up of books filled with lively and interesting new releases, a key element in keeping alive your students' active participation in reading.

In theory, the concepts and ideas behind guided reading are readily apparent and usually supported by middle school teachers. However, when the idea of implementing this model is broached with middle school language arts teachers, the elephant in the room begins to appear—time. As Julie began to develop the concepts and ideas that eventually became this program, the first thing she had to address with other teachers was the time commitment. Teachers who supported our ideas initially expressed concerns: "This is a great concept. But how am I supposed to manage 100 students and develop the lessons necessary to teach from several books?" These types of comments did not come from uncaring, undedicated teachers. They came from committed teachers who simply could not see a way to manage the time commitment this program would require. Teachers' concerns about time are understandable.

The beauty of guided reading is its adaptability. The guidelines we present in this chapter provide resources that will enable you to customize your reading instruction to serve the needs and interests of your students. Knowing how to manage the classroom, structure the flow of the day, teach mini-lessons, guide students in selection of individual reading, and effectively gather them to a table ready to learn is important, but it is in those small guided reading groups where this program comes alive. In that setting you will play different roles depending on the needs of the students. Initially, you may lead the discussions, helping students with selected comprehension challenges. As the students become more proficient in group discussion, your role becomes that of a facilitator modeling for students behaviors that effectively sustain the discussion. Finally, you may become an observer of the group, taking advantage of opportunities to assess how well your students are developing as readers, listeners, speakers, and writers.

Choosing Good Books for Guided Reading

Choosing good books for guided reading is the most important decision you will make in regards to increasing students' reading comprehension. You'll want to choose books that have literary merit, yet are both accessible and interesting for your students. Determining what you mean by "good" books may be an important starting point for your decision making. As we have selected books for our guided reading units, we have used several questions to guide our decisions. These questions are shown in the checklist on the following page.

Checklist for Choosing Books

**Questions to Ask Yourself When
Choosing Books for Guided Reading Units**

_____ Is this book at the readers' instructional level?

_____ Does the book contain high quality language and writing style?

_____ Has the book won any awards?

_____ Does the book contain learning opportunities that match your instructional goals?

_____ Does the book represent diverse gender, racial, cultural, and socioeconomic groups in positive ways?

_____ Will this book fit with two or three other books to create a cohesive unit?

_____ If there is an identifiable common theme or genre to group the books together, does this book fit in with the developing, advanced, and grade level concepts to allow for differentiation?

_____ If this book was selected as part of a specific genre, are all the elements of the selected genre present in the story? If not, is the book still relevant, even if it is not a "pure" reflection of the genre?

Series Books and Students' Interests

Creating lifelong readers is one of the broadest but most important language arts standards. Although we may observe our students' developing interest in reading while they are in our classes, we cannot realistically ever know if they will all become lifelong readers. Of course, our greatest concern is for those students who are the most reluctant to read. One approach to helping struggling students enjoy reading is getting them excited about a story. Books from series often help with this problem. Select series books for the guided reading units.   Struggling readers need opportunities to gain confidence. Conquering a challenging book from a series often marks a turning point for these students.   Reading the next releases in a series can support the students' confidence.   The previously struggling readers can step into the second book in a series already comfortable with the main character, the formula of the plot, and the author's language. Because of this familiarity, they read the book more quickly, which supports their fluency and they become more confident as readers. They come to see themselves as experts in the series, which encourages them to discuss the book more deeply in conversations and analyze the book more effectively in their writing.

Julie chose the book *Sammy Keyes and the Hotel Thief* (Van Draanen 1998) for her guided reading mystery unit because the book was recommended by many of her students.   The book was one of the most "checked-out" mystery books in the school library and it was the first book in a long series.   Many of the students enjoyed the book and upon seeing that it was part of a series, moved on to the next book.   In particular, one of Julie's English Language Learner students enjoyed the story so much that he "devoured" the entire series of Sammy Keyes books in only two months.   By meeting the standard of creating a lifelong reader by selecting an interesting book, and by providing this student with the analytical and strategic ability to comprehend a challenging text in the meeting groups, the guided reading program had created a situation where a student was continually getting better by voluntarily reading (Ivey and Broaddus 2001).

Another seemingly obvious factor in choosing guided reading books is student interest level.   Try to choose books that your students will enjoy and look forward to reading, but realize it is not always possible to meet their specific requests.   Students know what they like to read, but they don't know what they *need* to read.   Popular books do not always equate to books filled with robust teachable points.   Allowing students to "weigh in" on the decision of what book they will read in the guided reading unit is a great idea.   However, it isn't always possible to include their choices all of the time—teaching points and budget factors have to be taken into account.

Although you can't always meet the wishes of your students, there are some ways to get their input. When thinking about pulling books together for a fantasy unit, Julie chose *The Dark Hills Divide* (Carman 2005) because several students had made a point to tell her how much they enjoyed the story. She didn't immediately go out and buy a set of the books; rather, she read the book first, and although she was not as enthusiastic about it as her students were, she analyzed the story for elements of the fantasy/mystery genre. Julie noticed that the book provided many teaching points that would deepen her students' understanding of symbolism and imagery, as well as plot twists that would make it an appropriately challenging book for many students. The story also contained many opportunities to reinforce the reading strategies of inferring, connecting, visualizing, and predicting. The book has a Lexile score of 990. After examining all of these factors, Julie selected the book and included it in her unit.

When piloting a new guided reading book, purchase only the minimum number of books you'll need for a group and share the books among your different classes. Seven books are just enough for a guided reading group of six students (with one teacher copy). Don't let the students take these particular books out of your classroom. This will allow you to use them for other guided reading groups in your other language arts classes.

The Dark Hills Divide was an excellent choice for Julie's students because they were challenged, and, in the end, they displayed a deeper understanding of the aforementioned literary devices. Her students connected to the characters and were so intrigued by the plot twists that most of them read the next book in the series for their self-selected reading. As a result of this first guided reading success, Julie taught this book several times to students with varying reading levels in order to see which group it would fit with best. In the end, she decided that it met the needs of the advanced readers very effectively and she continues to teach this book to her advanced group.

Patience and Flexibility Are Key

Even if you follow the above guidelines when choosing a book for guided reading, it is possible that your students' enthusiasm may still be lacking. Sometimes it takes time and patience to find the right book. Even though students may not like a story you choose and you find it difficult to keep them engaged, you can still ensure that the students learn the literary objectives by focusing on reading strategies that help them "get through" the books. In a perfect scenario, you would like to have books that you enjoy teaching and your students enjoy reading. Such is not always the case, as Mark's experience illustrates.

Mark chose the book *Indian Captive* (Lenski 1995) that was on sale for 95 cents in a book club offer. Based on its Lexile score, the book seemed appropriate for his students. It was a Newbery Honor book about Native American life in the frontier and seemed to portray this group in an accurate and positive way. Mark also chose the book because it was an adventure book with a female protagonist and most of the other adventure books that he was teaching were about "boys lost in the woods." Although the price was what initially drew him to it, he thought about other factors in making this book choice.

What Went Wrong?

As Mark met with his guided reading groups, he found that the students complained that the plot dragged in many places. He noted this and realized that he obviously read much more fluently than his students did and therefore got through the long detailed parts more quickly. For the slower readers, the parts that dragged, *really* dragged. In re-visiting the book with a clearer perspective of what his students thought about it, he knew that if he pushed on with the book, which was his first instinct, the students were likely to stop reading altogether or make a best effort and complete only part of the assignment.

The options were either to abandon the book for the group—a choice which provided challenges because he had created no plans for an alternate book and the class was weeks into the unit—or to find a way to support the students through *Indian Captive*. To solve this dilemma, Mark opted to provide an oral detailed summary of the long, boring sections and then focus the student reading on the parts that were interesting. Using this method, Mark was able to meet the educational goal of analyzing the text for the elements of adventure, as well as focusing on other literary devices, such as story elements and internal conflict.

Since his students did not enjoy this story, he feared that his selection of the book might have turned them off of the adventure genre entirely. Later in the year he taught *Touching Spirit Bear* to get these students interested in the adventure genre again. Although this particular misadventure did cost Mark some time and energy, it fortunately did not cost him a lot of money. The books, which cost less than a dollar in the first place, were resettled in his classroom library, where an interested student occasionally reads a copy.

Mark first purchased *Coraline* (Gaiman 2004) in 2004, but decided not to teach it in a guided reading group because he thought the book was dreadfully scary (it gave him nightmares). Four years later, when the movie was released, several students noticed the *Coraline* books in his room and requested to read them. Their engagement was high and Mark took advantage of it and taught the book in a guided reading unit as part of a fantasy/horror genre. Due to the timing of the release of the movie, he had great success with it.

Philosophy of the Guided Reading Units

Our goal is to increase our students' reading comprehension by creating a realistic reading experience while teaching students the skills they need to analyze selected texts within a specified genre. Reading a "real" book, discussing it, and thinking about the book in a small setting is representative of what happens in the real world. People read books and talk about them. This is what happens in life and what should also happen in the classroom. However, in the classroom setting, the acquisition of skills is essential and lessons must be designed to serve that purpose.

Each genre unit is constructed so that the early lessons are more detailed and directive. The units begin with mini-lessons (see Chapter 7) which provide the framework for both literary and literacy objectives. These lessons, which we usually teach to the whole class, provide support for students' understanding as they first experience a new text. As students participate in the small group meetings, we gradually release the responsibility for reading comprehension to them. Sometimes student ideas and themes will begin to drive the conversations in the guided reading groups. Unless the conversation is veering off topic, we think it is counter-productive to "reel" the students in. Rather, it is quite natural to expect that your students' guided reading group discussions will take on a life of their own. You are the guide for the group and this role should be reflected in the way in which your lessons are planned.

We want to encourage students to take ownership of their literacy experiences. This ownership is evidenced by an increased student leadership and decreased teacher direction as we work through the books. In essence, the teacher's role is fluid. The role of the teacher may begin as a "transmitter of knowledge," but then shift to a "facilitator of discussion" and continue on to a "quiet observer." However, as any teacher knows, these roles can be played out at any time with different student groups or individuals. Often, just when you think that the students are on their way to greater independence, some

When differentiating for ELL and special education students, including students who fall on the spectrum of autism, we've found these students perform better when asked *direct* comprehension questions that have *concrete* answers. These questions seem to depart from a constructivist approach but in reality, these are modifications that actually differentiate instruction, so that *all* students can be accommodated and experience success in the guided reading meeting. Using sentence stems or front-loading vocabulary allows these students to participate in higher-level critical thinking.

happenstance event will reverse the whole process. Of course, that is one of the joys and challenges of teaching adolescents!

Planning a Guided Reading Unit

Guided reading provides great flexibility in designing lesson plans. If the book selection process has provided a piece of young adult literature that is rich in content, offers deep and complex characters, contains many elements of genre, and contains broad far-reaching themes, the options on what to teach are limitless. Ideally, Julie likes to go to the text with a broad idea of what strategies and literary elements a particular set of students needs and mine the text for the strongest teaching points. The book typically lends itself to specific teaching points relevant to both literary and literacy standards. Obviously, the students will also be reading the book, and their interests will influence what and how the book is covered. This interplay between the book, the students, and the teacher, within the broad contexts of the standards, is the ideal way to approach lesson planning.

Standards-driven

There are times, however, when a specific concept must be taught. At these times, Julie approaches the text in a more focused manner. For example, if Julie must focus on a standard that requires the students to come to an understanding of the role of "mood" and how it impacts the setting, then she will go to the text looking for the author's application of this specific concept. Even if the book lends itself to teaching another idea, she will work hard to ensure that the concept of "mood" is covered while also not giving up on the opportunity to teach the other concepts that the book presents. Curriculum standards offer an array of topics, and individual standards may contain several topics. Consider these examples from the *Common Core State Standards for English Language Arts and Literacy* (2010), shown in figure 9.1. (See Appendix D for a complete listing of the Common Core State Standards English Language Arts, Grades 6–8.)

Fig. 9.1. Excerpt from *Common Core State Standards* for Craft and Structure, Grades 6, 7, and 8 (2010)

Grade 6: Standard 4

Determine the meaning of words and phrases as they are used in a text, including figurative and connotative meanings; analyze the impact of a specific word choice on meaning and tone.

Grade 7: Standard 4

Determine the meaning of words and phrases as they are used in a text, including figurative and connotative meanings; analyze the impact of rhymes and repetitions of sounds (e.g., alliteration) on a specific verse or stanza of a poem or section of a story or drama.

Grade 8: Standard 4

Determine the meaning of words and phrases as they are used in a text, including figurative and connotative meanings; analyze the impact of specific word choices on meaning and tone, including analogies or allusions to other texts.

Each of these standards contains several focal points. You will likely find comparable examples in the curriculum standards for your state or district. To meet the standards and to capitalize on the literary aspects of a selected book, your lesson planning must have priorities—ones that meet the standards, ones that accommodate the characteristics of the selected book, and others that serve the needs and interests of your students. In this way, you will be providing your students with quality experiences that further their literary and literacy development. By identifying the teaching points from the book first and capturing the opportunities to teach the concepts that present themselves, we lessen the chance of taking a narrow approach to the text. Such an approach allows for the creation of robust lessons where the features of the book guide application of the standards, rather than the other way around.

Some books may not contain material suitable to developing a particular literary concept. The lack of one particular opportunity to teach a standard in a specific book should not exclude that book from consideration as part of your guided reading collection. The concept can always be taught in a mini-lesson. For the students reading a book where this concept is not present, the mini-lesson provides an introduction. If the concept has been presented in a book other students are reading, the mini-lesson serves as a refresher.

In language arts, the standards are recursive. That is, we do not simply teach the theme once, then say, "Okay, let's move on and never mention it again." Rather, the literary concept of *theme* is revisited many times within a guided reading unit as well as during the school year until the students have eventually mastered it. In fact, theme is a topic repeated across grade levels in many sets of standards. As you plan your units, you can ensure that activities are designed to revisit and reinforce critical literary concepts and literacy strategies.

Framing questions that would lead to natural-sounding guided reading discussions was another objective that Julie kept in mind as she developed her units. It is important to allow students to create meaning from the text they read, so most of the questions should be open-ended to allow for further commentary from the students. With this said, discussions do not always work out the way you plan. Many factors go into having a natural discussion, such as time of day, day of week, when lunch is scheduled, and so forth. There are certainly times when you will have to be very directive with your students and the meeting will seem more like a question-answer session. However, care should be taken to ensure that your questioning doesn't come through as an interrogation of the students on the finer points of the story. As long as you know this is not your ideal guided reading meeting and continue to prompt your students to respond to each other thoughtfully, it is acceptable to occasionally ask directive questions to pull an answer or two from them. With effective questioning, students will be prompted to have open dialogue about the book and will eventually have in-depth conversations that will lead to deeper understanding.

A Continuum of Reading Development

The guided reading unit consists of several parts, each of which is intended to meet students' proficiencies as they develop. When Julie created her units, she noticed a pattern of student reading development across the three middle grades. Figure 9.2 represents our observations of a continuum of reading strategies from basic through advanced levels. This pattern of growth served as a broad guideline as we developed our units. Although the reading strategies are handled in a recursive manner, we tended to focus more on the strategies toward the basic level of the spectrum for our students in lower grades or at a developing reading level.

Fig. 9.2. Continuum of Reading Strategies

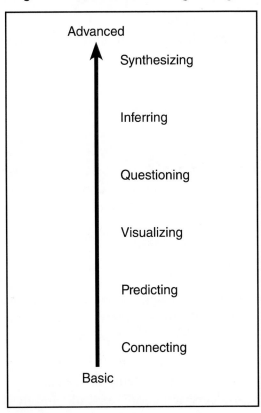

"…being in groups with other thinkers shapes our thinking as we shape the thinking of those around us. As students try to think deeper and move to analysis, critique, and more critical conversations, they not only make their own thinking more sophisticated, but also impact the minds of those with whom they discuss."

(Gilles 2010)

We use reading strategies to frame our units so that we help students learn how to pay attention to certain aspects of the text. By noting comprehension challenges within a book, we are able to identify reading strategies necessary to understanding the content. You can choose to teach the strategy in a mini-lesson or you can structure your questions to enable students to apply the strategy. Of course, the discussion in the small group will reveal the extent to which individual students are able to apply the strategy. As students progress through the higher-grade levels, they need to learn to develop a deeper understanding that requires purposeful planning and prompting by the teacher (Harvey and Goudvis 2000; Fisher, Frey, and Lapp 2010).

Components of the Guided Reading Unit

Within each unit we use three different books, selected to meet the differing levels of student reading achievement in our classes. Based on our assessment findings, we consider the students to be developing readers, grade level readers, and advanced readers, and assign them books appropriate to their reading levels. We analyze each novel to determine its instructional appropriateness. We review the novels to identify teaching points that align with the language arts curriculum standards and text features that might pose comprehension challenges for the students. A critical part of planning is developing effective questions that enable students to move from basic understanding to deep interpretation of the selection. The format of questions can determine how students will find the answers and the nature of those answers, or the levels of comprehension needed:

- Right there in the text—only one answer is possible

- Ideas in the text combined with personal knowledge, including experience with other texts—usually one answer is correct, but on occasion several responses might be appropriate

- Individual personal experience relevant to the text but not based on anything specific in the text—many answers are possible and reveal the students' abilities to respond critically to a text.

The question formats and relationship to comprehension levels can be described as *text explicit*, *text implicit*, and *experience-based*. We strive to provide open-ended questions that will prompt students to converse with one another in the guided reading meetings. However, we recognize that pre-planned questions don't always lead to the type of discussion in which students probe deeply into the meaning of the story. In those situations, the art of teaching comes into play—you have to be responsive to what is happening with the students.

The components we include in planning a guided reading unit are described in the chart on the following page.

Components of a Guided Reading Unit Plan

Component	Purpose
Book Overview	• Identify literary devices • Identify sources of potential comprehension challenges • Establish teaching points that align with curriculum standards • Establish framework for mini-lessons
Chapter Summaries	• Short notes about the content of each chapter • Serve as a reminder about key ideas in each chapter • Reference source for the teacher during guided reading meetings
Author's Craft	• Focus on literary elements contained in the novel; for example, theme, foreshadowing, flashback, symbolism, figurative language, plot, setting, and character development • Basis for developing questions to guide student discussion during guided reading meetings • Develop questions to accompany each chapter or grouping of chapters as appropriate

Components of a Guided Reading Unit Plan *(cont.)*

Component	Purpose
Comprehension Challenges	• Focus on content features that might challenge students' comprehension; for example, text features, and organizational patterns such as cause-effect, comparison-contrast, and problem-solution • Focus on vocabulary that is essential to understanding and appreciating the story • Consider these aspects in the context of selected literary devices; for example, understanding the vocabulary used in figurative language • Develop questions that will enable students to use a range of reading strategies to interpret the story • Questions used as pre-teaching resources to help frame students' understanding of key concepts in the story
Mini-lessons	• Focus on critical teaching points for literary devices and literacy strategies • Introduce the genre to the whole class • Introduce critical teaching points to the whole class • Review as needed for student groups
Reading Strategy: Connecting	• Questions that prompt students to use previous knowledge from their own experiences, knowledge of the world, and ideas from other texts to support and extend their comprehension
Reading Strategy: Questioning for Understanding	• Questions that can be answered by referring to specific passages or features of the text • Prompt "right there in the text" responses
Reading Strategy: Inferring	• Questions that invite students to construct meaning by thinking about a particular moment/event in the story and combine it with personal knowledge
Reading Strategy: Predicting	• Questions that prompt students to think about what they notice from a certain piece of text and make educated guesses about what will happen next • These questions are vital in helping students anticipate aspects of character and plot development

Components of a Guided Reading Unit Plan *(cont.)*

Component	Purpose
Reader's Notebook	• Questions that provide opportunities for students to think and write more deeply about the text • Students maintain a notebook for each novel they study; this notebook may also include commentary about their self-selected books

Overview of Resources We Use in Our Guided Reading Programs

We have developed units for these genres: adventure, fantasy, historical fiction, mystery, narrative poetry, and science fiction. Although we have listed the genres in alphabetical order, we do not intend to suggest that this is the order in which the units should be taught. The order you choose to teach the genres is based on the needs and interests of your students. For example, students may be more familiar with adventure and mystery stories, so selections from those categories might be appropriate for study early in the school year. However, many students are enthusiastic about science fiction, so that genre might be a suitable starting point for such a group. Appendix E contains an overview of the novels we have used for each of the genres. For each genre, we provide these details:

- Description of the genre

- Lexile score for each novel and student group for which the novel was selected

- Introduction to the novel

- Teaching points for the novel

- Comprehension challenges present in the novel

Our experience teaching guided reading units has expanded our knowledge of effective practice and enhanced our awareness of the potential of adolescents to become engaged and enthusiastic readers. We hope that you have similar positive experiences with your students.

Reflections on Adolescent Literacy

"Our students need to hear us talk about good books ('good' in terms of how the students define *good*), which means we teachers have to be avid readers of the kinds of books our students will read. If your enthusiastic booktalk encourages one student to read that book, that student is likely to do two things: 1) ask you for another recommendation, and 2) tell other students about the book. Moreoever, you can't just talk about the book. Those books have to be available in your classroom. Every classroom should have its own mini-library, with a variety of good books that students can see, touch, open. They need to be given some classroom time to read at least a few pages every so often (the more often the better)—just a taste, to see if they like that book."

—*(Gallo 2010)*

"Ice Cream/I Scream for YA Books," the article from which this quotation is taken, presents a metaphorical comparison of Don Gallo's two loves—ice cream and young adult books. He asks how any teacher of language arts or reading can *not* love YA books.

1. What are your views about contemporary YA books? Which titles appeal to both you and your students? Which titles appeal to the students, but not so much to you?

2. Some YA books generate controversy. Consequently, teachers are sometimes hesitant to use such books in their classrooms. What experiences have you had with "controversial" YA books?

3. What has been your experience with the novels Julie and Mark used in their guided reading progam? Of these, which did you find most effective in promoting your students' interest in reading?

Think back to your initial impressions of the guided reading model that you formed from reading the Introduction and Chapter 1 of this book.

4. How have your impressions changed as you read more chapters? In what ways has the authors' passion for inspiring adolescents to become lifelong readers influenced your thinking about teaching and learning?

5. In adopting the guided reading model for your classroom, what topics would you pursue with colleagues? What topics would you like to delve into more deeply if you had a chance to have a conversation with Julie and Mark?

Assessment Resources

Assessment Using Grade-level Text

Another way to measure students' reading levels is to see how they fare with authentic text—the passages they will encounter in the curriculum. Although a relatively obvious approach, this type of assessment requires more work. When using this method in previous years, we selected a series of passages that present increasing challenges to the student. In assessing a seventh grader, for example, we begin with a typical seventh grade text that should take about two to three minutes to read. By listening to the student read and following along with a copy, we can get a good feel for fluency and start identifying reading strengths and areas of development for each student. Going through the individual assessments helps alleviate some of the facelessness that comes with having a 150-student load.

Listening to a student read is a fantastic way to get a quick idea regarding his fluency. Following this reading up with a few quick questions sets the stage for a teacher to begin to deeply understand what is going on in a student's head when he or she is reading. This process is not as neat and packaged as the computer testing models, nor does it give you a specific number like a Lexile score to statistically analyze student reading growth. However, it does provide baseline information that allows the teacher to begin the process of creating the homogeneous groups that are the core of a guided reading program. When selected reading followed by specific questioning is done for an entire class, or groups of classes, trends emerge that indicate group deficiencies. These trends help a teacher guide instruction as part of a whole group.

Reading Comprehension Evaluation Checklist

The following Reading Comprehension Evaluation Checklist is designed to be specifically used with the reading selections above. It is a tool designed to help streamline the initial assessment process. To start, complete the biographical data at the top. If you are interested in getting a specific fluency score for the student, make a copy of the reading so you can mark on it. As the student reads his or her copy, place a mark by the words they struggled with. To arrive at an accuracy score, simply divide the number correct by the total number of words (noted on the top of each reading). This will give you the percentage of words read correctly. Record this under the "Accuracy" line.

To calculate the fluency, take the number of words correct and divide it by the total number of seconds the student took to read. Multiply this number by 60 and you will have words correct per minute (wcpm). For example, if a student read 290 words correctly in two minutes and 25 seconds, you would divide 290 by 145 seconds. The result is 2.0 words per second. Multiply this by 60 and you get 120 wcpm. Record this under the "fluency" line.

Although you should note any errors the student makes on your copy of the reading and record the time read, performing the actual calculations should wait until the student has left as you will need to be focusing on the comprehension and reading strategies questions.

At the end of each reading selection there are a series of questions to ask the student. During your initial assessment with the student, we suggest you ask every question. Each question is either a summarizing question or a question designed around a reading strategy. Not all strategies are covered for each reading selection. The higher-level reading selections are more focused on the higher-level strategies. When a student answers a question, assess the student's answer. If the student did very well and seemed to fully understand, a plus sign (+) should be recorded on the line next to the strategy. If the answer shows some depth of understanding, a check mark should be inserted (✓). If the student struggled, a minus sign (–) would be inserted. Some teachers have added ✓⁺ and ✓⁻ to give a greater sense of accuracy. Others have used numbers. Whatever rating scale you prefer is fine, it is just important to be consistent from student to student and over time.

Use the "Initial Observations" line to record some qualitative observations about the students reading.

- Did the student seem confident in reading, or did the student seem tentative?

- Were the answers given quickly, or did they require some time to think through?

- How much prompting from the teacher was required?

The ongoing notable observation is a small place for the teacher to record what they are noticing about the student after the initial grouping.

- Do they seem to be performing better than the assessment would show?

- Are they struggling to get deeper and broader concepts for the full novel? Essentially, this space can be used for any ongoing observations that are informative about the student.

Finally, it is important to remember that although this is designed as an initial assessment tool, it can be used at any time through the year. Although you will get most of your information about your student as a reader from the small group work you do with them, a focused one on one assessment can be used to support (or possibly refute) your observations from the small groups.

Reading Comprehension Evaluation Checklist

Name_____

Hour _____**Grade**_____**Date** _____

Title of Text _____

Fluency

Words correct per minute (wcpm) _____

Accuracy Percent correct

(Divide the number of words the student reads correctly by the total number of words.)

Reading Strategy Application (+, ✓, or –)

Summarizing: _____   Visualizing: _____

Questioning: _____   Predicting: _____

Connecting: _____   Inferring: _____

Initial observations: _____

_____

_____

_____

Initial grouping recommendation: _____

Ongoing notable observations:

_____

_____

Instructions for the Reading Assessment

Many of the questions are open-ended. There are few right and wrong answers. The main idea behind these questions is to get a feel for the students' ability to apply reading strategies and interact with the text. A percentile score of the questions answered correctly will not necessarily be helpful. We suggest an overall rating of plus (+) if the student answers the question significantly better than his peers, a check (✓) if it is about average and a minus (–) if the answers present some deficiencies.

The main goal of this type of reading assessment is to provide information to the teacher to initially place the students into appropriate groups. Sometimes this becomes very clear after one reading. It is not necessary to rank a student or develop a specific quantifiable score, so there is no reason to have a student read a second selection once the teacher has the information necessary to place a student, the assessment is over. For example, if a teacher has a class where only five students perform above grade level, there is no need for further assessment. These students would constitute the advanced group. If, on the other hand, a class presents 10 students who score well above grade level, a second assessment using a higher-level text *may* be helpful to further sort these students into two appropriate groups.

Feel free to pursue follow-up questions. If an answer is partial or unclear, ask clarification questions. Again, the goal is not to mark answers correct or incorrect, but to assess a student's abilities and development. Often, this requires one or more follow-up or clarification questions.

These readings and questions are typically used for initial placement into a group. As the year progresses, embedded and ongoing assessments (arising out of group meetings and individual students' work) are typically more informative.

Accuracy can be assessed by tracking the student reading, and noting the words missed to calculate the total number correct. Divide this by the total number of words read to get a percentage correct. If this is below 95 percent, further remediation may be required.

Calculating the total words read correctly and dividing this number by the number of seconds spent reading can assess fluency. This number multiplied by 60 will give the words correct per minute. If a student is significantly below the other students who are assigned to a particular book, ensure that accommodations are made for this student (this may include assigning this student their personal copy of the book, reducing other homework assignments, or allowing access to an audio version).

Examples of Reading Assessments

Book: *Stargirl* by Jerry Spinelli (pp. 22–23)

Reading Level: Lexile 590, total word count: 299

Introduction to the Reading: Stargirl is a new student who has recently come to her new high school. This describes one of her first nights at a football game.

Passage:

Except this night. This night, Stargirl Caraway was on the field with them (the marching band). As they played, rooted in their places, she pranced around on the grass in her bare feet and long lemon-yellow dress. She roamed from goalpost to goalpost. She swirled like a dust devil. She marched stiffly like a wooden soldier. She tooted an imaginary flute. She pogoed into the air and knocked her bare heels together. The cheerleaders gaped from the sidelines. A few people in the stands whistled. The rest—they barely outnumbered the band—sat there with "What is this?" on their faces.

The band stopped playing and marched off the field. Stargirl stayed. She was twirling down the forty-yard line when the players returned. They did a minute of warm-up exercises. She joined in: jumping jacks, belly whomps. The teams lined up for the second half kickoff. The ball perched on the kicking tee. She was still on the field. The referee blew his whistle, pointed to her. He flapped his hands for her to go away. Instead she dashed for the ball. She plucked it off the tee and danced with it, spinning and hugging and hoisting it into the air. The players looked at their coaches. The coaches looked at the officials. The officials blew their whistles and began converging on her. The sole policeman on duty headed for the field. She punted the ball from the field and ran from the stadium.

Everyone cheered: the spectators, the cheerleaders, the band, the players, the officials, the parents running the hot dog stand, the policeman, me. We whistled and stomped our feet on the aluminum bleachers. The cheerleaders stared up in delighted surprise. For the first time, they were hearing something come back from the stands.

Questions for *Stargirl*:

1. What is happening in this reading section? (Summarize to show basic comprehension)

2. What things did the girl do? (Summarize to show basic comprehension)

3. Describe the most interesting moment in this reading; get a picture in your head and let me know what you see. (Visualization)

4. Have you ever seen anything like this? Do you know someone like this girl? Have you ever read a story about another character like Stargirl? (Connections)

5. As you finish this reading, are you wondering about anything? Do you have any questions? (Questioning)

6. What is going to happen to Stargirl? (Prediction)

7. Describe Stargirl's personality. Why do you think she would do something like this? (Inferring)

~~~~~~

Book: *The Watsons Go to Birmingham—1963* by Christopher Paul Curtis (pp. 12–13)

Reading Level: Lexile 1000, total word count: 299

Introduction to the Reading: In this scene, Kenny, the narrator, is scraping ice off of the family car with his older brother Byron. Kenny has heard Byron mumbling something, but Kenny is trying to ignore Byron.

Passage:

I took a little rest and Byron was still calling my name but sounding like he had something in his mouth. He was saying, "Keh-nee! Keh-nee! Hel'...hel'...!" When he started banging on the door of the car I went to take a peek at what was going on.

By, (Byron) was leaned over the outside mirror, looking at something in it real close. Big puffs of steam were coming out of the side of the mirror.

I picked up a big, hard chunk of ice to get ready for Byron's trick.

"Keh-nee! Keh-nee! Hel' me! Hel' me! Go geh Momma! Go geh Mom-ma! Huwwy uh!"

"I'm not playing, Byron! I'm not that stupid! You'd better start doing your side of the car or I'll tear you up with this ice ball."

He banged his hand against the car harder and started stomping his feet. "Oh, please, Keh-nee! Hel' me, go geh Mom-ma!"

I raised the ice chunk over my head. "I'm not playing. By, you better get busy or I'm telling Dad."

I moved closer and when I got right next to him I could see boogers running out of his nose and tears running down his cheeks. These weren't tears from the cold either; these were big juicy crybaby tears! I dropped my ice chunk.

"By! What's wrong?"

"Hel' me! Keh-nee! Go geh hel'"

I moved closer. I couldn't believe my eyes! Byron's mouth was frozen on the mirror! He was as stuck as a fly on flypaper!

I could have done a lot of stuff to him. If it had been me with my lips stuck on something like this he'd have tortured me for a couple of days before he got help. Not me though, I nearly broke my neck trying to get into the house to rescue Byron.

Questions for *The Watsons Go to Birmingham—1963*:

1. What is happening in this reading section? (Summarize to show basic comprehension)

2. What did Kenny notice that finally convinced him Byron was in real trouble? (Comprehension)

3. Describe the most interesting moment in this reading; get a picture in your head and let me know what you see. (***Teacher:*** *prompt for more details if not offered by student.*) (Visualization)

4. Describe the relationship between Kenny and Byron. (Inferring)

5. Describe Kenny. What is he like? (Inferring)

6. As you finish this reading, are you wondering about anything? (Connections)

7. Do you have any questions? (Questioning)

8. What is going to happen to Byron? (Prediction)

~~~~~~

Book: *Downsiders* by Neal Shusterman (pp. 54–55)

Reading Level: Lexile 1110, total word count: 294

Introduction to the Reading: In this scene, Lindsay, a teenage girl, just found a strange boy in her bedroom and she sprayed him with mace. Todd is Lindsay's older brother.

Passage:

It was all a bit embarrassing for Lindsay. Certainly there was that first moment of triumph as she depressed that little aerosol knob—but as she watched him bounce around the room like a pinball going for bonus points, her sense of empathy kicked in. Clearly this person was not right in the head—one need only look at the way he was dressed: sewn shreds of fabric, a vest made of old paper clips or something of that sort. But it wasn't only his clothes. There was some strangeness in his eyes-or what she had seen of his eyes before temporarily blinding them. He wasn't quite...normal. At least not normal in the way that Lindsay had come to understand it.

Now after bouncing off the TV, the wall and the bedpost, he lay on his hands and knees coughing and groaning, completely helpless at her feet, and suddenly Lindsay felt a bit foolish standing there, as if she had used a cannon to kill a fly. Todd burst into the room not a second later, with a few spectators behind him.

"What's going on up here? Who is that? What's he screaming about?"

Lindsay did her best to explain the situation in twenty-five words or less, and Todd, for the first time in his life, complimented her. "Good for you, Lindsay," he said. But somehow a compliment from Todd didn't make her feel any better about this unpleasant state of affairs.

As Todd wedged his foot beneath the wailing boy's ribs, flipping him over onto his back like a turtle, Lindsay began to feel even more sorry for him. She was warned about this in self-defense class. Never feel sorry for an attacker, because it makes you the victim twice. Remember— sympathy kills.

Questions for *Downsiders*:

1. What is happening in this reading section? (Summarize to show basic comprehension)

2. What is Lindsay's impression of the boy on the floor? (Comprehension)

3. Describe the relationship between Lindsay and Todd. (Inferring)

4. Describe Lindsay; what do you think her personality is like? (Inferring)

5. What does it mean when the author writes "...her sense of empathy kicked in"? (Inferring)

6. What does the author mean when he writes "Never feel sorry for an attacker, because it makes you the victim twice. Remember—sympathy kills"? (Inferring)

7. Are you wondering about anything? Do you have any questions? (Questioning)

8. What is going to happen to the boy on the floor? (Prediction)

Guided Reading Record Sheet

The guided reading record sheet is designed to support the teacher in managing meeting with multiple groups at the same time. It provides a way for planning the next meeting, reviewing the focus of previous meetings, and assessing students' work in the meeting. Write the name of each student in the group in the left column. In the next columns to the right, record some information about each student. Use a checkmark (✓) to represent when the student was prepared and ready for the group and a zero if they were not, or insert a number to represent a grade for that group meeting. Some teachers give points for each group meeting, for example 0–3 total points possible, representing "totally unprepared" (zero), "partially completed the reading" (1), "reading done but failure to participate in the meeting" (2), or "reading complete and student fully participated in the meeting" (3).

In the "Meeting Focus" column, make a quick note of the meeting focus of that particular group. This becomes particularly helpful when meeting with multiple groups reading the same book over the course of a day. Different groups may focus on different topics. This is a nice quick reminder for the teacher about what was discussed at the last meeting.

Finally, in the "Observations and Comments" section, make notes about individual students or note trends in the group. This may be a place to make a small note that the group needs extra support on understanding a nuanced plot or that it might be time to push the group to understanding a difficult symbol.

Guided Reading Record Sheet

Book Title _____

Prepared? (*X* Yes); (*0* No)

Student Name	M1	M2	M3	M4	Meeting Focus	Next Meeting Date

Observations and Comments:

M = Meeting

Student Comprehension Resources: Thinking Sheets

Name: _____

Understanding Characters

Character: _____

To fully understand why characters do the things they do, pay attention to how the character is described by the author. A character is revealed through his or her actions, feelings, goals, conversations, and appearance.

Directions: Choose one character and chart the following evidence from the book that reveals the character's personality.

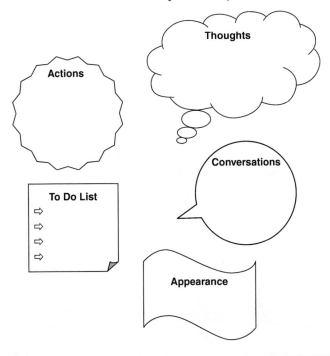

Name: _____

Character Changes

Characters change as a result of the experiences they have throughout the story. Just like us, they grow in response to the lessons they learn or the challenges they face.

Directions: Think about the main character(s) in your book and describe ways in which these individuals change and why.

1. Describe the character's personality in the beginning of the story. Be sure to include at least three personality traits in your description.

   _____

   _____

   _____

   _____

2. Describe the event that you think causes the character to change. What specifically happens?

   _____

   _____

   _____

   _____

3. How does the character change? Be specific and use evidence from the book to support your claim.

   _____

   _____

   _____

   _____

   _____

Name: _____

Discovering New Worlds

Book Title: _____

Authors use a variety of techniques to help readers figure out the meaning of unfamiliar words they encounter when they read. Context clues embed the definition of the word in the same sentence or provide an example of the word in the text that surrounds it. Sometimes other words in the sentence compare to or contrast with the unfamiliar word.

Directions: Make a list of the unfamiliar words you encounter as you read, including the page number. Then draw the word and define it in your own words. If you're unsure about the definition, discuss it with another group member. For an added challenge, name the type of context clue the author used.

Unfamiliar Word_____**Page**_____ **My Definition** _____ _____ **Picture:**	**Unfamiliar Word**_____**Page**_____ **My Definition** _____ _____ **Picture:**
Unfamiliar Word_____**Page**_____ **My Definition** _____ _____ **Picture:**	**Unfamiliar Word**_____**Page**_____ **My Definition** _____ _____ **Picture:**

Name: _____

Using Context Clues to Learn New Words

Context clues are words or phrases that help readers understand new words. The clues usually appear in the sentences before and after the unfamiliar word.

Directions: When you reach a word that you do not recognize, reread the words before and after it. Then make a logical guess about the meaning based on what is happening in the story.

Book Title: _____

Unfamiliar Word	Words or Phrases that Provide a Clue	My Logical Guess

Understanding New Words by Drawing the Meaning

Directions: Define each word in your own words and draw your understanding of that word in the space provided.

Word: _____

Definition: _____

_____

_____

Word: _____

Definition: _____

_____

_____

Word: _____

Definition: _____

_____

_____

Word: _____

Definition: _____

_____

_____

Name: _____

Story Elements

Book Title: _____

Author: _____

Characters: List the main character and supporting characters. Write a short description for each one.

Main Character

```
┌─────────────────────────────────────────┐
│                                         │
│                                         │
│                                         │
│                                         │
└─────────────────────────────────────────┘
```

Supporting Characters

```
┌──────────────────┐   ┌──────────────────┐
│                  │   │                  │
└──────────────────┘   └──────────────────┘

┌──────────────────┐   ┌──────────────────┐
│                  │   │                  │
└──────────────────┘   └──────────────────┘
```

Problem: Identify the challenge the characters face.

_____

_____

_____

_____

Solution: How is the problem resolved?

```
┌─────────────────────────────────────────┐
│                                         │
│                                         │
│                                         │
└─────────────────────────────────────────┘
```

Imagery

Authors create images in readers' minds by making unusual comparisons with words.

Directions: When you are reading, identify an instance of where the author made unusual comparisons and describe what you think it means. Then draw the image that you visualized.

Comparison: _____

_____

Visualized:

The unusual comparison occurs: _____

_____

_____

I think it really means… _____

_____

_____

Bonus:

When authors compare two unlike things, it is called using *figurative language*. What type of figurative language was used to create this image?

Circle one: metaphor   simile

Name: _____

Noticing Hints and Clues: Making Predictions to Solve a Mystery

Authors of mystery novels include clues to make the story more interesting. These clues (sometimes called hints) help the reader follow along in the story and try to solve the mystery.

Directions: When you are reading, write down any hint or clue that you find and what you think it means. Make a prediction about what will happen next in the story based on your interpretation of the clue.

Clues That I Noticed (page number)	My Interpretation and Prediction

Name: _____

Understanding the Message of the Story: Theme

The theme of a story is considered to be the author's main message about human nature, life, or society. The theme is often a timeless and universal message.

Directions: After reading the story, write about what you think the main message, or theme, of the story is. Describe the message in your own words and provide evidence by including details from the story to support your statement.

Book Title: _____

I think the author's message (theme) is:

_____

_____

_____

_____

_____

Evidence from the Story that Supports My Thinking

Evidence/page number	**Evidence/page number**
_____ _____ _____	_____ _____ _____
Evidence/page number	**Evidence/page number**
_____ _____ _____	_____ _____ _____

Name: _____

How the Setting Influences Character Actions

The setting of a scene in a story refers to the time and place in which a story takes place. The setting influences what a character does or thinks and can provide readers with insight into the attitudes of the characters that live during that time.

Directions: If you are reading, describe the scene and include the evidence you find to support what you found.

Book Title: _____

Character(s): _____

Details About the Scene	What Is the Mood of the Scene?	What Happened?
Time: _____ Evidence: _____ _____ Place: _____ Evidence: _____ _____	Description: _____ _____ _____ Evidence: _____ _____ _____ _____ _____	

Write a paragraph that describes how the setting of this scene influenced the actions of the character you chose.

_____

_____

_____

_____

Understanding Symbolism

A symbol is something that stands for something else. A symbol can be an object or an action that represents an idea or a feeling.

Directions: As you are reading, write down any symbolic objects or actions and describe what they mean and how they help you understand the story.

Symbolic Object or Action	I think it means...	This helps me understand the story better because...

Sample Mini-lessons

Mini-Lesson Plan: Elements of the Mystery Genre

Purpose of Lesson: Introduce characteristics of the mystery genre

Target Students: 6th, 7th, or 8th grade

Literary Focus: Elements of the mystery genre

Procedure:

- Tell the students to come up with the characteristics (elements) that most mysteries have in common.

- Guide the students in a general conversation about what they already know about mystery. Ask them to share any mystery shows or books they have read or seen recently. (Expect a large number of responses relating to televised crime shows. Be sure to manage this to keep the discussion on topic.)

- Read a selection or two from Donald Sobol's *Two-Minute Mysteries* or *More Two-Minute Mysteries*.

- Guide the students in solving the mystery (the solutions are in the back of the book).

- Ask the students to reflect on the mysteries they shared and the mysteries you read. Have the students think about what elements seemed to be present in the mysteries. Post the students' list on chart paper.

Student Task:

As you read your own mystery novel, think about the elements of mystery that appear in your book. In order to support your understanding of these elements, name at least two examples of the elements and be ready to share with the class.

Assessment:

Listen to student responses to check for understanding and read students' responses in their reader's notebooks.

Example of a List:

---

mystery—usually a crime of some sort or an unanswered question

clues—hints and facts that help resolve the mystery

suspects—characters who may have committed the crime

investigator—person trying to solve the mystery

red herrings/distractions—characters or information that the author gives the reader in order to put the reader on the wrong path while trying to solve the mystery.

plot twists—Unexpected changes to the plot that surprise the reader.

Note: The students may not suggest red herrings/distractions or plot wists. If they do not, add them to the list with explanations and examples.

Mini-Lesson Plan: Symbolism

Purpose of the Lesson: Introduce the concept of symbolism

Target Students: 6th, 7th, or 8th grade

Literary Focus: A symbol is something that stands for something else. When authors write stories, they often use symbols in the story to make it more interesting to read.

Procedure:

- Show students pictures of everyday symbols and ask them what they mean. Show a bathroom sign, a peace sign, and a stop sign, each without the lettering. (This can effectively be presented in a slide show format.) Explain that symbols may be things that we can touch, but they represent things that we cannot touch.

- Read a short piece of text that contains a symbol. For instance, in the novel *Crossing Jordan,* the fence that was built by the main character's father represents the racial barrier the girls have to overcome to be friends. The fence is *tangible,* so we can touch it. The concept of racial barriers is *intangible,* meaning that we cannot touch it.

Student Activity:

Students will read their guided reading novel or self-selected novel for 25–30 minutes, identify at least one symbol, and attempt to explain what they think it stands for. Students will write one paragraph about their symbol in their reader's notebooks. They should be prepared to share it at the end of class.

Assessment:

Listen to student responses and read notebook entries to verify their understanding.

Mini-Lesson Plan: Procedures for an Effective Guided Reading Meeting

Purpose of the Lesson: To have an effective guided reading meeting

Target Students: 6th, 7th, or 8th grade

Literacy Focus: Learning to listen to each other

Procedure:

- Begin by asking students, "What makes you feel frustrated when you are talking in a group?"

- Ask students to imagine six people having dinner together. Ask students to imagine what it would be like if each member raised his or her hand to speak. Then have them imagine what it would be like if all members spoke at once.

- Lead students through a brainstorming session to establish guided reading meeting norms.

- One possible solution would be to give specific hand signals when asking to be recognized in the guided reading group setting. Students can use two fingers to signal that they have a related thought, or one thumb up for a new topic. (This works well with 6th grade students.)

- Another solution for older students would be to wait for a pause in the conversation, much like one does at a dinner table and then "piggyback" or paraphrase what the last person said before commenting on their idea.

- Read a short piece of text to the students. It works well if it can be displayed on the overhead.

Student Activity:

Ask students to talk to their table mates for 3–5 minutes to discuss the text with each other using the technique agreed upon. Be sure everyone has enough time to share. Call on individual students and have them relay the thought shared by a table member rather than their own thoughts.

Assessment:

Listen to student responses. Observe students in guided reading meetings and discuss with them the effectiveness of the procedures. Use the list of discussion guidelines the students developed to help them evaluate their discussions.

Example List:

I feel frustrated when...

...people interrupt.

...people do not relate their thoughts to my comments.

...people do not listen and just repeat exactly what I said.

...one person takes over or monopolizes the conversation.

...a person does not complete his/her reading and is not prepared.

...a person does not speak.

Mini-lesson Plan: Visualizing Setting in Fantasy Novels

Purpose of the Lesson: Helping students understand the role of setting in creating the mood of a story; guiding them in visualizing story settings

Literacy Focus: Visualizing the setting in fantasy novels. What do we mean when we say "the setting creates the mood of the story"?

Target Students: 6th, 7th, or 8th grade

Procedure:

- When we read a novel, the author often describes the setting in great detail so the reader can visualize where the story is taking place. When this happens, the reader is transported to that place and understands the story better. As I read this passage to you, visualize the setting and sketch it in your reader's notebook.

  > *The Dark Hills Divide*
  >
  > The sun had set, and the lamps glowed above the streets with sharp yellow spears, one every twenty feet on both sides along our way. Illuminated by the soft light, the cobblestone paths made for a dreamy stroll. As we rounded each new corner we were greeted by another twisting row of lamps, houses, and small storefronts. Some of the doors were painted bright blue or purple, but the houses themselves, crammed tightly together, were all whitewashed stone.

- After five minutes, allow students to share their drawings.

- Ask students what feeling they get when they read about this setting. Do they feel like it is a welcoming place, or a scary place? Do they feel anxious or calm when they read it? Why or why not?

Student Task:

As you read your own fantasy book, choose a setting to sketch. Be ready to share it with the class and tell how the setting made you feel.

Extension for Guided Reading Groups:

Build on this concept and explain that the mood of any particular setting will give the reader an idea as to what might happen next in the story. You might ask students to describe the mood and predict what will happen next.

Assessment:

Review student sketches.

Mini-lesson Planning Form

Lesson Plan Title: _____

Lesson Purpose: _____

_____

Target Students: _____

Literary Focus (curriculum standard):

_____

_____

or, Literacy Strategy Focus (curriculum standard):

_____

_____

Procedure: _____

_____

_____

_____

_____

_____

_____

_____

_____

_____

_____

_____

_____

Mini-lesson Planning Form *(cont.)*

Student Activity: _____

_____

_____

_____

_____

Assessment: _____

_____

Example:

Common Core State Standards for English Language Arts, Grades 6–8

Appendix D

Key Ideas and Details			
Standard	Grade 6	Grade 7	Grade 8
1	Cite textual evidence to support analysis of what the text says explicitly as well as inferences drawn from the text.	Cite several pieces of textual evidence to support analysis of what the text says explicitly as well as inferences drawn from the text.	Cite the textual evidence that most strongly supports an analysis of what the text says explicitly as well as inferences drawn from the text.
2	Determine a theme or central idea of a text and how it is conveyed through particular details; provide a summary of the text distinct from personal opinions or judgments.	Determine a theme or central idea of a text and analyze its development over the course of the text; provide an objective summary of the text.	Determine a theme or central idea of a text and analyze its development over the course of the text, including its relationship to the characters, setting, and plot; provide an objective summary of the text.
3	Describe how a particular story's or drama's plot unfolds in a series of episodes as well as how the characters respond or change as the plot moves toward a resolution.	Analyze how particular elements of a story or drama interact (e.g., how setting shapes the characters or plot).	Analyze how particular lines of dialogue or incidents in a story or drama propel the action, reveal aspects of a character, or provoke a decision.

Common Core Standards for
English Language Arts, Grades 6-8 *(cont.)*

Craft and Structure			
Standard	**Grade 6**	**Grade 7**	**Grade 8**
4	Determine the meaning of words and phrases as they are used in a text, including figurative and connotative meanings; analyze the impact of a specific word choice on meaning and tone.	Determine the meaning of words and phrases as they are used in a text, including figurative and connotative meanings; analyze the impact of rhymes and other repetitions of sounds (e.g., alliteration) on a specific verse or stanza of a poem or section of a story or drama.	Determine the meaning of words and phrases as they are used in a text, including figurative and connotative meanings; analyze the impact of specific word choices on meaning and tone, including analogies or allusions to other texts.
5	Analyze how a particular sentence, chapter, scene, or stanza fits into the overall structure of a text and contributes to the development of the theme, setting, or plot.	Analyze how a drama's or poem's form or structure (e.g., soliloquy, sonnet) contributes to its meaning.	Compare and contrast the structure of two or more texts and analyze how the differing structure of each text contributes to its meaning and style.
6	Explain how an author develops the point-of-view of the narrator or speaker in a text.	Analyze how an author develops and contrasts the points-of-view of different characters or narrators in a text.	Analyze how differences in the points-of-view of the characters and the audience or reader (e.g., created through the use of dramatic irony) create such effects as suspense or humor.

Common Core Standards for
English Language Arts, Grades 6-8 *(cont.)*

	Integration of Knowledge and Ideas		
Standard	**Grade 6**	**Grade 7**	**Grade 8**
7	Compare and contrast the experience of reading a story, drama, or poem to listening to or viewing an audio, video, or live version of the text, including contrasting what they "see" and "hear" when reading the text to what they perceive when they listen or watch.	Compare and contrast a written story, drama, or poem to its audio, filmed, staged, or multimedia version, analyzing the effects of techniques unique to each medium (e.g., lighting, sound, color, or camera focus and angles in a film).	Analyze the extent to which a filmed or live production of a story or drama stays faithful to or departs from the text or script, evaluating the choices made by the director or actors.
8	(Not applicable to literature)	(Not applicable to literature)	(Not applicable to literature)
9	Compare and contrast texts in different forms or genres (e.g., stories and poems; historical novels and fantasy stories) in terms of their approaches to similar themes and topics.	Compare and contrast a fictional portrayal of a time, place, or character and a historical account of the same period as a means of understanding how authors of fiction use or alter history.	Analyze how a modern work of fiction draws on themes, patterns of events, or character types from myths, traditional stories, or religious works such as the Bible, including describing how the material is rendered new.
10	By the end of the year, read and comprehend literature, including stories, dramas, and poems, in the grades 6–8 text complexity band proficiently, with scaffolding as needed at the high end of the range.	By the end of the year, read and comprehend literature, including stories, dramas, and poems, in the grades 6–8 text complexity band proficiently, with scaffolding as needed at the high end of the range.	By the end of the year, read and comprehend literature, including stories, dramas, and poems, at the high end of grades 6–8 text complexity band independently and proficiently.

Appendix E

Guided Reading Unit Resources

Adventure Genre

Adventure novels provide teachers with a multitude of opportunities to deepen students' comprehension. Because many adventure novels are centered on the act of survival by the main character, you couldn't ask for a better opportunity to teach students how characters change and grow in response to the challenges they face. Adventure novels also lend themselves to lessons about understanding characters' actions and analyzing relationships among characters. These novels also provide ample opportunities for students to discover new vocabulary words.

Novels Selected for the Adventure Unit

We have used three novels for our guided reading groups. The novels, along with Lexile scores and assigned student reading groups, are summarized below. For each novel we provide an overview of the story, identify the teaching points that align with curriculum standards, and indicate some comprehension challenges.

Novel	Lexile Score	Student Group
The Music of the Dolphins (Hesse 1996)	550	developing readers
Touching Spirit Bear (Mikaelsen 2001)	680	grade level readers
The Hero (Woods 2002)	990	advanced readers

The Music of the Dolphins

Introduction to the Novel

The Music of the Dolphins is an atypical adventure story about a young Cuban girl's attempt to survive in the human environment rather than a story about the main character trying to survive in a wild environment. The main character was a victim of a boat crash when she was just four years old. She has been living on a remote island off the coast of Florida for about eight years, being cared for by a family of dolphins. One day, she is spotted by an observation plane and is rescued and taken away from the only family she has ever known. The story reveals what it is like for Mila to become "human" and her need to stay "dolphin."

Teaching Points

- Understanding elements of the adventure genre

- Comprehension strategy: making inferences

- Identifying and analyzing story elements: plot structure, setting, and climax

- Exploring characters' actions and motivations

Comprehension Challenges

- Even though this is a fictional story, students need to keep in mind there are many documented and legendary stories in which children have been found being raised by feral animals; for example, the legend of the twins Romulus and Remus who were saved by a wolf. You can easily research other examples on literary websites and provide students with some background knowledge of feral children. This background will help students suspend their disbelief as they read the story.

- The author uses italics to denote Mila's inner dialogue. The text changes to standard font when she is actually speaking. Readers will notice the text is large and very simple at the beginning of the book. It becomes increasingly smaller as the story proceeds to show Mila's acquisition of the English language.

- This book has several text features that contribute to building the plot and providing insight into the character. The newspaper article about Mila's rescue is written at a higher Lexile level than the other parts of the story. You may want to read this piece of text aloud and have the group follow along during the first meeting.

Touching Spirit Bear

Introduction to the Novel

Touching Spirit Bear is a story about a very angry 15-year-old boy named Cole Matthews, who has been living in a circle of abuse. He has learned not to trust anyone and has become a violent bully. Unfortunately, Cole's anger pushes him over the edge and he beats up another boy so badly that the boy suffers permanent physical and emotional injuries. Cole is given a choice between going to prison or taking part in Circle Justice, a Native American tradition of justice. Circle Justice involves self-reflection, repenting, and personal healing within a solitary environment. Being extremely motivated to stay out of prison, Cole chooses to be a part of Circle Justice and finds himself banished to a remote Alaskan island. However, during his first days there, a mysterious bear mauls him. Now, no one can save Cole unless he chooses to save himself first.

Teaching Points

- Understanding elements of the adventure genre

- Understanding characters' actions and motivations

- Understanding flashback and how and why authors use this device to move the story along

- Analyzing symbolism as it appears in the story

Comprehension Challenges

- The author switches between present time and past time almost seamlessly. Consequently, the students must be mindful of transition words and the literary device of flashback.

- Symbolism plays an important part in the development of this story. Students will need to understand how the author uses this literary device to give readers insights into the characters' feelings and actions.

The Hero

Introduction to the Novel

The Hero is a story about Jamie, a 14-year-old boy who lives in Union, Idaho, near the Payette River with his parents and six-year-old sister, Marie. It's the summer of 1957 and Jamie plans on building a raft with his older cousin, Jerry. However, Jamie's father forces him to include another boy, Dennis Leeper, in the plans to build the raft. Dennis is an unpopular and lonely boy whom no one really likes because his father has a reputation of being mean and unreasonable. Jerry dislikes Dennis and makes him the target of hostilities. When the raft is completed the boys are eager to take it out on the river. However, before they realize what is happening, all three boys are faced with a dangerous situation. They find themselves careening down the river on a raft without any paddles. The river is filled with dams and waterfalls. What will happen to the boys in the end? Who will be the hero?

Teaching Points

- Understanding elements of the adventure genre

- Identifying and analyzing story elements: plot structure, setting, and climax

- Understanding characters' actions and motivation

- Understanding the literary device of foreshadowing

- Understanding figurative language: simile and metaphor

Comprehension Challenges

- The author uses the literary device of foreshadowing, which gives readers indirect hints about an event to come. Students will have to be able to make predictions based on unconnected observations that the author embeds in the story to move the action along.

- The author uses figurative language to convey images. Students will have to be able to visualize these images as presented by similes and metaphors.

Fantasy Genre

We can't think of a more engaging genre for students in sixth, seventh, and eighth grades. Although the popularity of fantasy novels has made it very difficult at times for a language arts teacher to get students to read anything else, we feel it's important to take advantage of their enthusiasm for the genre to teach them certain literary devices. Fantasy provides opportunities to teach students how to identify and analyze story elements, including setting, mood, and conflict; build on their understanding of characters' actions and relationships with other characters; and to learn new vocabulary using context clues. Distinguishing fantasy from fact and fiction is another intriguing aspect of working with this genre.

Novels Selected for the Fantasy Unit

We have used three novels for our guided reading groups. The novels, along with Lexile scores and assigned student reading groups, are summarized below. For each novel we provide an overview of the story, identify the teaching points that align with curriculum standards, and indicate some comprehension challenges.

Novel	Lexile Score	Student Group
Artemis Fowl, Book 1 (Colfer 2002)	600	developing readers
A Wrinkle in Time (L'Engle 1962)	770	grade level readers
The Dark Hills Divide (Carman 2005)	940	advanced readers

Artemis Fowl, Book 1

Introduction to the Novel

This novel is about Artemis Fowl, a 12-year-old boy who is a genius and a criminal mastermind. Although Artemis is extremely wealthy and wise beyond his years, he still has a child-like interest in fairies and the mythical creatures of the underworld. Using high-tech equipment and the help of Butler, his trustworthy protector, Artemis sets out to do what no one has ever done: steal the fairies' golden treasure. This story is full of tricks and mind-bending twists that you'll never see coming.

Teaching Points

- Understanding elements of the fantasy genre

- Identifying and analyzing story elements: plot structure, climax, and setting

- Understanding characters' actions, motivations, and relationships with other characters

- Using context clues to understand specialized vocabulary

Comprehension Challenges

- The author uses specialized vocabulary for the fantasy world; for example, "lower elements" refers to the world where all the fairies, gnomes, trolls, and dwarves live.

- Some passages are written in poetic form.

- The concept of "altered consciousness" is central to some events in the novel. Students will need to be able to identify time relationships and how these are signaled in the text.

A Wrinkle in Time

Introduction to the Novel

This novel is a classic fantasy-adventure story of good versus evil. A young girl, Meg Murry, finds out that her imperfections are actually her strengths when she goes on an adventure with Charles Wallace, her genius younger brother, and Calvin, her friend. With the help of three magical beings, Mrs. Witch, Mrs. Who, and Mrs. Whatsit, the children set out to rescue Meg and Charles Wallace's father from the evil clutches of IT and save the universe.

Teaching Points

- Understanding elements of the fantasy genre

- Identifying and analyzing story elements: plot structure, climax, and setting

- Understanding characters' actions and motivations

- Identifying and analyzing figurative language

- Identifying the theme of the story

- Understanding symbolism and how it enhances the theme of the story

Comprehension Challenges

- The story is written in third-person narrative

- The narration moves between the past and the present as Meg's thoughts are revealed

- The author uses inner dialogue to present Meg's thoughts

- Symbolic language is used; for example, Fortinbras, Happy Medium, tesseract

The Dark Hills Divide

Introduction to the Novel

This fantasy-mystery story is about Alexa Daley, a very curious 12-year-old girl. Alexa is the daughter of the mayor of a city called Lathbury, which is one of the three major cities in the walled kingdom Land of Elyon. Each summer, Alexa accompanies her father to the annual meeting in Bridewell, the capital city governed by Warvold, the man who built the wall around the kingdom. Alexa's mother stays in Lathbury to govern the city during her husband's absence.

Because Alexa is the daughter of a mayor, she is allowed certain perks, such as staying in the luxurious Renny Lodge, the only building in the entire kingdom that is taller than the wall. On her first day there, she breaks an important law as she stands on a window ledge and looks through a stolen and illegal spyglass that she "borrowed" from her mother. In doing so, she catches a glimpse of something moving on the other side of the wall. This fuels her curiosity and she begins a personal quest to discover who or what lives on the other side. She has spent her lifetime wondering what was outside the wall. This summer the opportunity to find out just what is out there will arise unexpectedly. Will Alexa be ready for the challenges she will face?

Teaching Points

- Analyzing the story for fantasy elements
- Recognizing and interpreting symbolism and foreshadowing
- Understanding mood and how it is conveyed
- Analyzing figurative language, including idioms
- Exploring the story theme as it is developed through symbolism, foreshadowing, and mood
- Identify author's use of clues to move the plot forward

Comprehension Challenges

- The first chapter contains a folk tale from India. Students will have to understand the moral of the tale and be able to relate this concept to events later in the story.

- A map of Elyon is provided near the beginning of the book. Students will have to be able to use this visual aid as they read the entire book.

- New characters are introduced as the plot develops. Students will have to be able to keep track of the characters and understand their roles in the development of the plot.

Historical Fiction Genre

Historical fiction can be one of the most powerful genres to support overall teaching. The stories are typically set in exciting times (for example, the Civil War, the Revolutionary War, World War II, the Civil Rights Movement, great migrations, and periods of immigration) or periods that seem to captivate young readers (for example, the Middle Ages, or the Age of Exploration). The immersion in these stories is deepened in many cases by the author's use of first person.

Good historical fiction takes these times long past and breathes new life into them. By creating characters of an age and a disposition that today's students can understand and empathize with, these novels bring important historical concepts to life in ways that no textbook ever could. This provides the opportunity to expand a student's reading ability while also building their overall knowledge of history.

Novels for the Historical Fiction Unit

We have used three novels for our guided reading groups. The novels, along with Lexile scores and assigned student reading groups, are summarized below. For each novel we provide an overview of the story, identify the teaching points that align with curriculum standards, and indicate some comprehension challenges.

Novel	Lexile Score	Student Groups
Chains (Anderson 2008)	700	developing readers
Code Talker (Bruchac 2005)	910	grade level readers
The Watsons Go to Birmingham—1963 (Curtis 1995)	1000	advanced readers

Chains

Introduction to the Novel

In historical fiction novels, authors present readers with a story that takes place during a specific period in history, usually during a significant event in that period. This novel takes place just before the American Revolutionary War breaks out and tells the story of a determined 13-year-old slave girl, Isabel, who was promised freedom by her owner. After her owner passes away, Isabel and her younger sister, Ruth, are sold to the Locktons, a very mean British couple. The Locktons actively disagree with the Patriots' agenda. They also treat Isabel and Ruth poorly. Will Isabel ever win freedom for herself and her sister?

Teaching Points

- Understanding features of historical fiction
- Identifying and analyzing metaphorical language
- Understanding differences in society between historical and contemporary times
- Understanding symbolism
- Understanding characters' actions and motivations

Comprehension Challenges

Likely the most challenging aspect that students will encounter in reading historical fiction is recognizing how the society in the story differs from their own. These differences are not just a matter of costume, food, and living accommodations. The differences are reflected in societal values and attitudes; for example, teaching slaves to read or allowing girls to attend school. Students need to understand that although the story is a fictionalized account of the characters' lives, the historical aspects of the story are (or should be) accurate.

Although the main character, Isabel, can read, she has not been formally taught. Consequently, she modifies and makes up words, sometimes using them in odd ways. Students should understand how Isabel's "approximations" help to convey the meaning that she was deriving from her reading.

Understanding something about the events during the period when the story is set enhances students' comprehension and appreciation of the story. They should know the time period of the Revolutionary War, what the war was about, the nature of society at that time, and the impact of the war on different groups of people.

Code Talker

Introduction to the Novel

Code Talker takes place during World War II. The story centers on Ned Begay, a 16-year-old Navajo boy. When Ned learns that the Marines are specifically recruiting Navajos, he lies about his age in order to enlist. He quickly becomes involved in a top-secret mission as a code talker. Navajo soldiers played an important role in sending coded messages during the fight against the Japanese military in the Pacific Theater. The events portrayed in this novel are indeed actual events from history told from Ned's point-of-view. The story begins in the current day, with Ned showing his grandchildren a medal he was awarded for his service during the war.

Teaching Points

- Understanding elements of the historical fiction genre
- Understanding symbolism
- Understanding flashback
- Understanding irony

Comprehension Challenges

- Navajo names and terms are used throughout the novel. Students should take note that the author always defines each Navajo word immediately after it appears in the story.

- Students should understand why the Navajo code talkers made such important contributions during the World War II.

- The author uses flashbacks to provide the story context and to develop characterization. Students will need to be able to recognize when the main character is in "flashback mode" and when he is not.

- The story reveals distinguishing aspects of Navajo culture. These examples provide opportunities to extend students' sensitivity to cultural beliefs different from those in their own communities.

- Students should have some understanding of the geography of the story setting.

The Watsons Go To Birmingham—1963

Introduction to the Story

This novel tells the story of an African American family living in Flint, Michigan, who take a trip to Birmingham, Alabama, at the height of the Civil Rights Movement and experience some of the threatening aspects of that time in the United States. The terrorism of the anti-civil rights movement is brought home as the family lives through the bombing of the 16th Street Baptist Church in Birmingham. The story is narrated by Kenny, a precocious and academically gifted elementary student. He describes his relationships with his brother Byron, his sister Joey, and his parents and their experiences at home as well as in Birmingham.

Teaching Points

- Understanding character development

- Understanding the theme of the story and how characterization contributes to development of the theme

- Understanding figurative language, including idioms, similes, and metaphors

- Analyzing the impact of historical fiction in creating awareness of what happens when "ordinary people" are involved in "extraordinary events"

Comprehension Challenges

- The author is known for using details to make readers sense that they are actually "living with" the characters. Students should recognize this technique as "bringing the reader into the scene" and be able to determine if such detail aids or hinders their understanding.

- The novel has many emotional scenes, which students should be able to visualize and analyze from the different perspectives of the adults and children in the family.

Mystery Genre

Students either seem to love mystery stories or be a little put off by them. As works of literature, the mystery genre sometimes gets a bad rap. Maybe it was the pulp fiction stories, or the cheesy cop stories that earned this reputation, but as far as current young adult novels go, the mystery genre is alive and well. The quest to solve a puzzle can draw a reluctant reader in and give them a motivation to read that isn't always there. The excitement and tension of an adolescent character caught up in a crime, or even a murder, can have a young teen zipping through hundreds of pages. Finally, the author who uses the mystery almost as a backdrop to the exploration of characters and core values can challenge the talented reader to think deeply while still providing a little bit of fun.

Another unique aspect of mystery that lends itself to teaching in middle school is that most novels follow the genre characteristics fairly closely. Regardless of setting or even character types, the mystery novel always provides a problem to be solved, clues, suspects, and an investigator. These consistent, common elements allow for great opportunities for whole group sharing among all levels of readers. Mystery novels provide opportunities to teach students how to adopt an investigative point-of-view, to be able to look at evidence, to observe details, to form predictions, and to evaluate the appropriateness of their predictions.

Novels for the Mystery Unit

We have used three novels for our guided reading groups. The novels, along with Lexile scores and assigned student reading groups, are summarized below. For each novel we provide an overview of the story, identify the teaching points that align with curriculum standards, and indicate some comprehension challenges.

Novel	Lexile Score	Student Group
Sammy Keyes and the Hotel Thief (Van Draanen 1998)	630	developing readers
Down the Rabbit Hole: An Echo Falls Mystery (Abrahams 2005)	680	grade level readers
The Boys of San Joaquin (Smith 2005)	950	advanced readers

Sammy Keyes and the Hotel Thief

Introduction to the Novel

Sammy Keyes and the Hotel Thief is the story of a spunky 13-year-old girl who manages to get herself into interesting predicaments due to her curiosity. She is a refreshing character who is unafraid to stand up for herself and to fight for what is right. Sammy lives with her grandmother because her own mother left her to pursue a career as a movie star. Sammy's lucky because she has a best friend, Marissa, who believes in Sammy no matter the circumstances. The adventure begins when Sammy witnesses a theft through her binoculars. Will she be able to catch the real thief, or will she be the one who is blamed?

Teaching Points

- Understanding elements of the mystery genre
- Identifying and analyzing story elements: plot structure, climax, and setting
- Understanding characters' actions and motivation
- Understanding how the author builds tension using the moment-by-moment technique
- Understanding the author's use of clues, including ones designed to sidetrack the reader (red herrings)

Comprehension Challenges

- The author uses figurative language extensively, which requires the reader to move beyond literal interpretation of the text.
- In reading a mystery, students should be prepared to identify clues that keep the reader on track as well as those the author uses to divert attention. Periodically, they should examine their predictions to determine how effectively they were able to distinguish credible clues from red herrings in making the predictions.
- This story is told in first-person narrative, a form that is likely quite familiar to most of the students.

Down the Rabbit Hole: An Echo Falls Mystery

Introduction to the Novel

Down the Rabbit Hole is a thoroughly intriguing story about a girl named Ingrid Levin-Hill, who is like many middle school girls. She plays soccer, hates math, loves acting in the theater, and has a passion for reading mystery stories about Sherlock Holmes. In many ways, she has a very average life living in Echo Falls with her parents, her annoying older brother, Ty, her quirky but lovable dog, Nigel, and her very stubborn grandfather. Ingrid is the last person one would expect to be involved in murder.

Teaching Points

- Understanding elements of the mystery genre

- Identifying and analyzing story elements: plot structure, climax, and setting

- Understanding characters' actions and motivation

- Understanding how the author builds tension using the moment-by-moment technique

- Understanding the author's use of clues, including ones designed to sidetrack the reader (red herrings)

Comprehension Challenges

- Distinguish between main characters and "flat" characters who are undeveloped but who provide insight to the main characters or help connect them to the resolution of the mystery.

- Interpret figurative language through visualization and illustration.

- Understand the symbolism of the expression "rabbit hole" (from *Alice in Wonderland,* where Alice's wild adventures begin when she falls down a rabbit hole).

The Boys of San Joaquin

Introduction to the Novel

The Boys of San Joaquin is a humorous mystery novel that is somewhat unusual. Paolo, the main character, is a 12-year-old boy from a large Appalachian-Italian family. The story is set in 1951 in Orange Grove City, California. Paolo sets out to solve the mystery behind a lost stash of money. But solving the mystery is only part of this story. While trying to discover the truth behind the stolen money, Paolo learns a lot about his family, his friends, and himself.

Teaching Points

- Understanding elements of the mystery genre
- Understanding characters' actions and motivations
- Recognizing clues and how the author uses these to advance the plot
- Understanding foreshadowing
- Understanding flashback
- Recognizing and interpreting figurative language

Comprehension Challenges

- The story begins with the main character, Paolo, telling the story as an adult, an older man who is remembering his childhood. Students will have to recognize flashback and the purpose it serves in developing the story.

- Students will have to interpret time relationships as reflected in the first-person narrative.

- The story has many characters who are described at the beginning of the book in a "character portfolio" written in Paolo's voice.

- Some dialogue is written in an Italian dialect. These passages are best read aloud to get the full impact of the grandfather's dialect.

- The story contains references to the internment of Japanese citizens during World War II. Students will need to understand the historical context as it relates to some characters in the novel.

- Students will need to recognize how various aspects of life in 1951 differ from the life they know today.

Narrative Poetry Genre

Narrative poetry is a great way to get students to appreciate and understand the many aspects of poetry while keeping them engaged in a (longer) story. We find that by guiding students through stories written in verse, they can more easily identify and understand figurative language and imagery because the story provides them with a larger context in a format they are more familiar with.

Narrative poetry presents topics and situations that are familiar to students from having read different types of novels such as historical fiction and realistic fiction. The familiarity of the narrative form helps overcome the antipathy that students often have toward poetry. Most middle school teachers have encountered the negative attitudes that many adolescents have about poetry. Using narrative poetry is an effective way to help students develop interest in this literary form.

Poems Selected for the Narrative Poetry Unit

We have used three narrative poems for our guided reading groups. The poems and assigned student reading groups are summarized below. For each narrative poem, we indicate the type of narrative, identify the teaching points that align with curriculum standards, and indicate some comprehension challenges.

Narrative Poem	Narrative Type	Student Group
Home of the Brave (Applegate 2007)	narrative fiction	developing readers
Out of the Dust (Hesse 1997)	historical fiction	grade level readers
Make Lemonade (Wolff 1993)	realistic fiction	advanced readers

Home of the Brave

Introduction to the Poem

Have you ever visited a new place and felt like an outsider? Can you imagine what it would feel like if you could never return home and had to live in a new place? Every day there are people coming to America to begin new lives. Everything is unfamiliar to them as they struggle to learn a new culture and a new language all at once. In this story, Kek, a young refugee boy from Sudan, comes to live in Minnesota to begin a new life. He is alone except for his aunt and cousin. His father and brother did not survive a brutal attack on his Sudanese village. He has not heard if his mother survived, but has not given up the hope that he will someday see her again.

Teaching Points

- Understanding the elements of narrative fiction poetry

- Understanding theme

- Understanding figurative language: similes, metaphors, and idioms

- Understanding characterization

- Understanding symbolism

- Responding to words and phrases that create feelings of empathy for the character and engage the reader in reflection

Comprehension Challenges

- Symbolism is an important device the author uses to reveal the connections the main character makes between his former life in Sudan and his new life in Minnesota.

- Students will need to analyze cultural differences and recognize how these impact the development of the story characters.

Out of the Dust

Introduction to the Poem

This poem is set in Joyce City, Oklahoma, in 1934. The soil is dry and dust storms are blowing in so frequently that sand mounds are covering the farms and killing the animals. Billie Jo is her parents' only child. She loves to play the piano like her mother, and is tall and stubborn like her father. When Billie Jo's mother dies in a terrible accident, her father, who is overcome with grief, will not talk about the death. Billie Jo has to find a way to help herself and her father make it through a very difficult time.

Teaching Points

- Understanding elements of historical fiction narrative poetry

- Understanding the concepts of symbolism, foreshadowing, and mood

- Understanding themes

- Responding to words and phrases that create feelings of empathy for the character and engage the reader in reflection

Comprehension Challenges

- Students will have to understand the time period in which the story is set and the impact of the conditions on people's lives.

- The story includes several characters who are revealed through the perspective of Billie Jo, the main character. Students will need to analyze the figurative language used to define these characters, as well as interpret what the use of figurative language reveals about Billie Jo.

- Mood is an important aspect of poetry. Students will need to understand how the author uses language to create mood.

Make Lemonade

Introduction to the Poem

Make Lemonade is the story of Jolly, a 17-year-old single mother of two who has had a difficult life. She is trying to make her life better for the sake of her children, but she doesn't know how. Jolly places an ad on a bulletin board for a baby-sitter. LaVaughn, a 14-year-old, answers the ad. LaVaughn, who is mature beyond her years, has an unshakeable goal to get out of the inner city by going to college. Through LaVaughn's help, Jolly's life begins to turn around.

Teaching Points

- Understanding elements of realistic fiction narrative poetry

- Analyzing aspects of character development, as these enhance the story theme

- Understanding figurative language

- Understanding symbolism

- Understanding flashback

- Responding to words and phrases that create feelings of empathy for the character and engage the reader in reflection

Comprehension Challenges

- The entire story is a flashback told from LaVaughn's point-of-view. She is the narrator of the story and is recalling the past.

- The story reveals many life difficulties of both characters. Students will need to make inferences about the challenges each character encounters.

- Symbolic language is used throughout the poem to convey such personal qualities as perseverance and making good choices.

Science Fiction Genre

Students today grow up with science fiction movies. Some of the most popular movies of all time (for example, *Avatar* and *Star Wars*) are science fiction. This context presents an opening to build on the students' previously established interests to expand their analysis of this complex genre. Although everyone seems to know that science fiction typically involves aliens and advanced technology, the genre also presents an opportunity to examine social commentary and complex interpersonal relationships and universal themes, concepts that are typically embedded in action-driven plots.

Novels Selected for the Science Fiction Unit

We have used three novels for our guided reading groups. The novels, along with Lexile scores and assigned student reading groups, are summarized below. For each novel we provide an overview of the story, identify the teaching points that align with curriculum standards, and indicate some comprehension challenges.

Novel	Lexile Score	Student Group
The Last Universe (Sleator 2005)	690	developing readers
Enchantress from the Stars (Engdahl 1970)	910	advanced readers
Downsiders (Shusterman 1999)	1100	grade level readers

The Last Universe

Introduction to the Novel

The Last Universe is a story about a family who lives in a very old house with a large, peculiar garden. The garden was designed by a great uncle who disappeared mysteriously many years ago. Susan, one of the main characters, takes care of her brother, Gary, who is confined to a wheelchair. Even since he became ill, Gary has requested that Susan take him into the garden for daily "walks." One day they discover something very strange happening in the garden. Susan is frightened and does not want to return, but Gary insists. Little do they know, their visits to the garden will change their lives forever.

Teaching Points

- Understanding elements of the science fiction genre

- Understanding characters' actions and motivations

- Understanding symbolism

- Understanding how the author creates suspense and uses it to advance the plot

Comprehension Challenges

- Science fiction stories involve readers in distinguishing between things and events that are real and imaginary. Readers must be able to suspend disbelief.

- Secrecy and inexplicable events carry the story, so students must be able to see how these factors contribute to development of the characters as well as the plot.

- Symbolic elements (for example, the concept "quantum" and the lotus flower) are present throughout the story. Students will need to understand what these symbols represent and how they contribute to the story.

Enchantress from the Stars

Introduction to the Novel

Enchantress from the Stars is a story about a girl, Elana, her father, and Everk, who are part of the Anthropological Service. Together they try to turn back a powerful invading Empire from a planet called Andrecia, where the story takes place. The setting is in a forest bordered by a river where, on the outskirts, there is a village populated by the Andrecians. The residents refer to the area as the "Enchanted Forest." The Imperial Service (the Empire) is the advanced society that is conquering the native Andrecians. The story questions the responsibilities of a more advanced society's actions toward a more primitive society. It is also about the ability of one person to make a real difference in the world.

Although this novel has a Lexile score of 910, the novel is more complex than this score indicates. The plot is complicated, the theme is sophisticated, and symbolic language is evident throughout the novel.

Teaching Points

- Understanding elements of the science fiction genre
- Understanding flashback
- Identifying and analyzing story elements including plot and setting
- Understanding symbolism
- Understanding characters' actions and motivations
- Understanding the theme of good versus evil
- Recognizing analogous relationships between the story and real events in the contemporary world

Comprehension Challenges

- The entire story is told through the literary device of flashback. Students will have to be aware of ways in which the author signals flashback and how the device affects the reader's understanding of the story.

- Characters speak telepathically. Students will need to recognize the text feature (italics) that signals this form of communication.

- The story has both a prologue and an epilogue. Students should understand the nature and purpose of these literary elements and why an author chooses to use them.

Downsiders

Introduction to the Novel

Downsiders is a story about Talon, a teenage boy who lives in Downside, which is a secret underground world beneath New York City. When Talon accidentally meets a teenage girl named Lindsay, who is a Topsider (from above the ground), their two worlds collide. Talon and Lindsay become friends and love blooms. However, the consequences for Talon's lack of discretion could be death.

Although this book has a Lexile score of 1100, it is not as difficult as the score might suggest. The plot is relatively simple and the language is not particularly difficult for students at grade level to manage.

Teaching Points

- Understanding elements of the science fiction genre
- Identifying and analyzing story elements including plot structure, setting, and climax
- Understanding characters' actions and motivations
- Analyzing the mood of the story
- Understanding how authors use foreshadowing and flashback

Comprehension Challenges

- The story opens with a prologue, a device that students may not have previously encountered.

- Students will need to understand the functions that flashback and foreshadowing play in advancing the story.

- Periodically, the author writes from the perspective of a narrator rather than from the perspective of the characters. Students will need to understand the role of a narrator and how the narration provides insights into the characters and events in the plot.

References Cited

Akhavan, N. *How to align literacy instruction, assessment, and standards.* Portsmouth, NH: Heinemann.

Allen, J. 2007. *Inside words: Tools for teaching academic vocabulary grades 4–12.* Portland, ME: Stenhouse.

Allington, R. 2001. *What really matters for struggling readers: Designing research-based programs.* New York: Longman.

Anderson, K. M. 2007. Tips for teaching: Differentiating instruction to include all students. *Preventing School Failure* 51 (3), 49–54.

Atwell, N. 2007. *The reading zone.* New York: Scholastic.

Beck, I. L. and M. G. McKeown. 1991. Conditions of vocabulary acquisition. *Handbook of reading research, Volume 2.* Eds. R. Barr, M. O. Kamil, P. Mosenthal, and P. D. Pearson, 789–814. White Plains, NY: Longman.

Beers, K. and R. E. Probst. 2011 (Spring). Connecting point-and-click kids to the power of novels: Reading literature as a 21st century skill. *PD Catalog-Journal.* Portsmouth, NH: Heinemann. Available at: http://www.heinemann.com/pd/journal/Beers_Probst_S11_PDCatalog-Journal.pdf

Biancarosa, G. and C. E. Snow. 2004. *Reading next—A vision for action and research in middle and high school literacy: A report to Carnegie Corporation of New York.* Washington, DC: Alliance for Excellent Education. Available at: http://www.all4ed.org/publications/ReadingNext/ReadingNext.pdf

Black, P., C. Harrison, C. Lee, B. Marshall, and D. Wiliam. 2004. Working inside the black box: Assessment for learning in the classroom. *Phi Delta Kappan* 86 (1)m 9–21.

Bomer, R. 1995. *Time for meaning: Crafting literate lives in middle and high school.* Portsmouth, NH: Heinemann.

Bradley, M. J. 2003. *Yes, your teen is crazy!* Gig Harbor, WA: Harbor Press.

Bromley, K. 2007. Nine things every teacher should know about words and vocabulary instruction. *Journal of Adolescent & Adult Literacy* 50 (7), 528–537.

Calkins, L. M. 1986. *The art of teaching writing,* 2nd edition. Portsmouth, NH: Heinemann.

Common Core State Standards for English Language Arts. 2010. http://www.corestandards.org/the-standards/ english-language-arts-standards (accessed June 2011).

Cunningham, P. M., and R. Allington. 1994. *Classrooms that work: They can all read and write.* New York: Harper Collins College.

Daniels, H. 2006. What's the next big thing with literature circles? *Voices from the Middle* 13 (4), 10–15.

Dweck, C. S. 2010. Even geniuses work hard. *Educational Leadership* 68 (1), 16–20.

Fisher, D., N. Frey, and D. Lapp. 2010. Real-time teaching. *Journal of Adolescent & Adult Literacy* 54 (1), 57–60.

Fountas, I. and G. S. Pinnell. 2001. *Guiding readers and writers.* Portsmouth, NH: Heinemann.

Frey, N., D. Fisher, and S. Everlove. 2010. Making group work productive. *Educational Leadership* 68 (1), 3. Online version available to ASCD members: http://www.ascd.org/publications/ educational-leadership/sept10/vol68/num1/toc.aspx

Gallo, D. 2010. Ice cream/I scream for YA books. *Voices from the Middle* 17 (4), 8–14.

Giedd, J. 2007. Private: Studying teens from the inside out: Inside the teenage brain. EarthSky interviews. http://www.pbs.org/wgbh/pages/frontline/shows/teenbrain/interviews/giedd.html (accessed April 2011)

Gilles, C. 2010. Making the most of talk. *Voices from the Middle* 18 (2), 9–15.

Graham, S. and M. A. Herbert. 2010. Writing to read: Evidence for how writing can improve reading. *A Carnegie Corporation Time to Act Report.* Washington, DC: Alliance for Excellent Education.

Graves, M. F. and S. Watts-Taffe. 2002. The place of word consciousness in a research-based vocabulary program. *What research has to say about reading instruction, 3rd edition.* Eds. A. E. Farstrup and S. J. Samuels, 140–165. Newark, DE: International Reading Association.

Harvey, S. and A. Goudvis. 2000. *Strategies that work: Teaching comprehension to enhance understanding.* York, ME: Stenhouse.

Heritage, M. 2007. Formative assessment: What do teachers need to know and do? *Phi Delta Kappan* 89 (2), 140–145.

Ivey, G. 1999. A multicase study in the middle school: Complexities among young adolescent readers. *Reading Research Quarterly* 34, 172–192.

Ivey, G. and K. Broaddus. 2001. "Just Plain Reading": A survey of what makes students want to read in middle school classrooms. *Reading Research Quarterly* 36 (4), 350–377.

Jackson, R. R. 2009. *Never work harder than your students & other principles of great teaching.* Alexandria, VA: Association for Supervision and Curriculum Development.

Jackson, Y., T. G. Johnson, and A. Askia. 2010. Kids teaching kids. *Educational Leadership* 68 (1), 60–63.

Kobrin, D. 2004. *In there with the kids: Crafting lessons that connect with students, 2ⁿᵈ edition.* Alexandria, VA: Association for Supervision and Curriculum Development.

Langer, J. A. 2009. Contexts for adolescent literacy. *Handbook of adolescent literacy research.* Eds. L. Christenbury, R. Bomer, and P. Smagorinsky, 49–64. New York: The Guilford Press.

Lattimer, H. 2003. *Thinking through genre.* Portland, ME: Stenhouse.

Lee, C. D. and A. Spratley. 2010. *Reading in the disciplines: The challenge of adolescent literacy.* New York: Carnegie Corporation of New York.

Lent, R. C. 2010. The responsibility breakthrough. *Educational Leadership* 68 (1), 68–71.

Marzano, R. J., D. J. Pickering, and J. E. Pollock. 2001. *Classroom instruction that works: Research-based strategies for increasing student achievement.* Alexandria, VA: Association for Supervision and Curriculum Development.

Marzano, R. J. 2003. *What works in schools: Translating research into action.* Alexandria, VA: Association for Supervision and Curriculum Development.

Marzano, R. J. 2004. *Building background knowledge for academic achievement.* Alexandria, VA: Association for Supervision and Curriculum Development.

Marzano, R. J. 2007. *The art and science of teaching: A comprehensive framework for effective instruction.* Alexandria, VA: Association for Supervision and Curriculum Development.

MetaMetrics. 2007. *The Lexile framework for reading.* http://www.lexile.com/m/uploads/maps/Lexile-Map.pdf (accessed February 10, 2011)

National Council of Teachers of English (NCTE). 2004. *A call to action: What we know about adolescent literacy and ways to support teachers in meeting students' needs.* Urbana, IL: National Council of Teachers of English.

National Council of Teachers of English (NCTE). 2006. *NCTE principles of adolescent literacy reform: A policy research brief.* Urbana, IL: National Council of Teachers of English. Available at: http://www.ncte.org/library/NCTEfiles/Resources/Positions/Adol-Lit-Brief.pdf

National Council of Teachers of English (NCTE). 2007. *Adolescent literacy: A policy research brief produced by The National Council of Teachers of English.* Urbana, IL: National Council of Teachers of English. Available at: http://www.ncte.org/library/NCTEFiles/Resources/PolicyResearch/AdolLitResearchBrief.pdf

National Council of Teachers of English (NCTE). 2008. *Writing now: A policy research brief.* Urbana, IL: National Council of Teachers of English. Available at: http://www.ncte.org/library/NCTEFiles/Resources/PolicyResearch/WrtgResearchBrief.pdf

National Middle School Association (NMSA). 2010. This we believe: Keys to educating young adolescents. *Position paper of the National Middle School Association. Executive Summary.* Westerville, OH: National Middle School Association. Available at: http://www.nmsa.org/portals/0/pdf/about/twb/This_We_Believe_Exec_Summary.pdf

National Reading Panel. 2000. *Report of the National Reading Panel: Teaching children to read. Report of the subgroups.* Washington, D.C.: U.S. Department of Health and Human Services, National Institutes of Health.

Oldfather, P. 1993. What students say about motivating experiences in a whole language classroom. *The Reading Teacher* 46, 672–681.

Pearson, P. D. and M. C. Gallagher. 1983. The instruction of reading comprehension. *Contemporary Educational Psychology* 8 (3), 317-344.

Pressley, M. 2002. Metacognition and self-regulated comprehension. *What research has to say about reading instruction, 3rd edition*. Eds. A. E. Farstrup and S. J. Samuels, 291–309. Newark, DE: International Reading Association.

RAND Reading Study Group. 2002. *Reading for understanding: Toward a R & D program in reading comprehension*. Arlington, VA: RAND. Available at: http://www.rand.org/pubs/monograph_reports/MR1465/MR1465.pdf

Rasinski, T. and N. Padak. 2005. *3-minute reading assessments: Word recognition, fluency, and comprehension: Grades 5–8*. New York: Scholastic.

Rief, L. 2003. Writing matters. *Voices from the Middle* 11 (2), 8–12.

Rog, L. and P. Kropp. 2001. Hooking struggling readers: Using books they can and want to read. *Reading Rockets*. Available at: http://www.readingrockets.org

Romano, T. 1987. *Clearing the way: Working with teenage writers*. Portsmouth, NH: Heinemann.

Ross, D. and N. Frey. 2009. Learners need purposeful and systematic instruction. *Journal of Adolescent & Adult Reading* 53 (1), 75–78.

Scholastic Professional Paper. 2008. *Lexiles: A system for measuring reader ability and text difficulty—A guide for educators*. New York: Scholastic. Available at http://teacher.scholastic.com/products/sri_reading_assessment/pdfs/SRI_ProfPaper_lexiles.pdf

Scholastic Reading Inventory technical guide. 2007. New York: Scholastic. Available at: http://teacher.scholastic.com/products/sri_reading_assessment/pdfs/SRI_TechGuide.pdf

STAR Reading: Understanding reliability and validity. 2007a. New York: Renaissance Learning. Available at: http://research.renlearn.com/research/pdfs/133.pdf

STAR Reading: Understanding STAR assessments. 2007b. New York: Renaissance Learning. Available at: http://www.loudincounty.org

Tomlinson, C. A. 2008. The goals of differentiation. *Educational Leadership* 66 (3), 26–30.

Worthy, J., G. Moorman, and M. Turner. 1999. What Johnny likes to read is hard to find in school. *Reading Research Quarterly* 34, 12–27.

YALSA Excellence in Nonfiction for Young Adults Award. 2008. American Library Association. http://www.ala.org/ala/mgrps/divs/yalsa/booklistsawards/nonfiction/nonfiction.cfm (Accessed June 21, 2011)

Yopp, R. H. and H. K. Yopp. 2007. Ten important words plus: A strategy for building word knowledge. *The Reading Teacher* 61 (2), 157–160.

Young Adult Literature for Guided Reading Units

Abrahams, P. *Down the rabbit hole: An echo falls mystery.* New York: HarperCollins, 2005.

Acampora, P. *Defining Dulcie.* New York: Dial, 2006.

Anderson, L. H. *Chains.* New York: Atheneum Publishers, 2008.

Applegate, K. *Home of the brave.* New York: Holtzbrinck Publishers. 2007.

Bruchac, J. *Code talker.* New York: The Penguin Group, 2005.

Carman, P. *The dark hills divide.* New York: Scholastic, 2005.

Colfer, E. *Artemis Fowl Book 1.* New York: Miramax/Hyperion Books, 2002.

Curtis, C. P. *Elijah of Buxton.* New York: Scholastic, 2009.

Curtis, C. P. *The Watsons go to Birmingham—1963.* New York: Delacorte Press, 1995.

Engdahl, S. L. *Enchantress from the stars.* New York: Atheneum Publishers, 1970.

Fleischman, P. *Seedfolks.* New York: Harper Trophy, 2004.

Fogelin, A. *Crossing Jordan.* New York: Peachtree Jr, 2002.

Gaiman, N. *Coraline.* New York: HarperCollins, 2004.

Hesse, Karen. *The music of the dolphins.* New York: Scholastic, 1996.

Hesse, Karen. *Out of the dust.* New York: Scholastic, 1997.

Higson, C. *Silverfin.* New York: Hyperion Book CH, 2009.

Hinton, S. E. *The outsiders*. New York: Speak, 1997.

Ho, M. *The stone goddess*. New York: Scholastic, 2005.

Konigsburg, E. L. *A view from Saturday*. New York: Atheneum, 1998.

L'Engle, Madeleine. *A wrinkle in time*. New York: Holtzbrinck Publishers, 1962.

Lenski, L. *Indian captive: The story of Mary Jemison*, New York: HarperCollins. 1995.

London, Jack. *White fang*. Mineola, NY: Dover, 1991.

Mazer, H. *A boy no more*. New York: Simon & Schuster Children's Publishing, 2006.

Mikaelsen, B. *Touching spirit bear*. New York: Harper Collins, 2001.

Shusterman, N. *Downsiders*. New York: Aladdin, 1999.

Sleator, W. *The last universe*. New York: Amulet Books, 2005.

Smith, D. J. *The boys of San Joaquin*. New York: Atheneum, 2005.

Sobol, D. J. *More two-minute mysteries*. New York: Scholastic, 1991.

Sobol, D. J. *Two-minute mysteries*. New York: Scholastic, 1967.

Spinelli, J. *Stargirl*. New York: Dell Laurel-Leaf, 2000.

Van Draanen, W. *Sammy Keyes and the hotel thief*. New York: Dell Yearling, 1998.

Werner, H. Only a dollar's worth. *Scholastic Read-Aloud Anthology*. Eds. J. Allen and P. Daley. New York: Scholastic, 1993.

Wolff, V. E. *Make lemonade*. New York: Henry Holt and Company LLC, 1993.

Woods, R. *The hero*. New York: Dell Yearling, 2002.

Young Adult Nonfiction for Guided Reading Units

Angel, Ann. *Janis Joplin: Rise up singing*. New York: Amulet/Abrams, 2011.

Barry, Lynda. *What it is*. Montreal, Quebec: Drawn and Quarterly, 2008.

Bartoletti, Susan C. *They called themselves the KKK: The birth of an American terrorist group*. New York: Houghton Mifflin Harcourt, 2011.

Clifford, Barry. *The lost fleet: The discovery of a sunken Armada from the golden age of piracy*. New York: William Morrow, 2003.

Cone, Maria. *Silent snow: The slow poisoning of the Arctic*. New York: Grove Press, 2005.

Erlbaum, Janice. *Have you found her: A memoir*. New York: Villard, 2008.

Hawk, Tony. *Between boardslides and burnout: My notes from the road*. New York: ReganBooks, 2002.

Hess, Elizabeth. *Nim Chimpsky: The chimp who would be human*. New York: Bantam, 2008.

Kot, Greg. *Ripped: How the wired generation revolutionized music*. New York: Scribner, 2010.

Lopez, Steve. *The soloist: A lost dream, an unlikely friendship, and the redemptive power of music*. New York: Putnam Adult, 2008.

Nelson, Kadir. *We are the ship: The story of Negro League Baseball*. New York: Jump At The Sun, 2008.

Polly, Matthew. *American Shaolin: Flying kicks, Buddhist monks, and the legend of Iron Crotch: An odyssey in the New China.* New York: Gotham Books, 2007.

Ralston, Aron. *Between a rock and a hard place.* New York: Atria Books, 2005.

Umrigar, Thrity. *First darling of the morning: Selected memories of an Indian childhood.* New York: Harper Perennial, 2008.

Wertheim, Jon L. *Blood in the cage: Mixed martial arts, Pat Miletich, and the furious rise of the UFC.* Boston: Houghton Mifflin Harcourt, 2009.

Recommended Reading

Appendix I

Allen, J. 2007. *Inside words: Tools for teaching academic vocabulary grades 4-12*. Portland, ME: Stenhouse Publishers.

Allen, J. and P. Daley. 2004. *Read-aloud anthology*. New York: Scholastic.

Atwell, N. 2007. *The reading zone*. New York: Scholastic.

Beck, I. L. and M. G. McKeown. 2006. *Improving comprehension with questioning the author*. New York: Scholastic.

Brassell, D. and T. Rasinski. 2008. *Comprehension that works: Taking students beyond ordinary understanding to deep comprehension*. Huntington Beach, CA: Shell Education.

Buss, K. and L. Karnowski. 2000. *Reading and writing literary genres*. Newark, DE: International Reading Association.

Daniels, H. and N. Steineke. 2004. *Mini-lessons for literature circles*. Portsmouth, NH: Heinemann.

Gainer, J. and D. Lapp. 2010. *Literacy remix: Bridging adolescents' in and out of school literacies*. Newark, DE: International Reading Association.

Harvey, S. and A. Goudvis. 2000. *Strategies that work*. York, ME: Stenhouse.

Johnston, P. H. 2004. *Choice words*. Portland, ME: Stenhouse Publishers.

Kajder, S. B. 2006. *Bring the outside in: Visual ways to engage reluctant readers*. Portland, ME: Stenhouse Publishers.

Kajder, S. B. 2010. *Adolescents and digital literacies*. Urbana, IL: National Council of Teachers of English.

Lattimer, H. 2003. *Thinking through genre: Units of study in reading and writing workshops grades 4–12.* Portland, ME: Stenhouse.

Nichols, M. 2008. *Talking about text: Guiding students to increase comprehension through purposeful talk.* Huntington Beach, CA: Shell Education.

Rasinski, T. V. and N. Padak. 2005. *3-Minute reading assessments.* New York: Scholastic.

Rasinski, T. V., N. Padak, R. M. Newton, and E. Newton. 2008. *Greek & Latin roots: Keys to building vocabulary.* Huntington Beach, CA: Shell Education.

Scott, R. M. 2008. *Knowing words: Creating word-rich classrooms.* Toronto, ON: Nelson.

Tomlinson, C. A. 1999. *The differentiated classroom: Responding to the needs of all learners.* Alexandria VA: Association for Supervision and Curriculum Development.

Tovani, C. 2003. *Do I really have to teach reading?* Portland, ME: Stenhouse Publishers.

———. 2000. *I read it but I don't get it: Comprehension strategies for adolescent readers.* Portland, ME: Stenhouse Publishers.